Praise fo

C000139009

Rooted in extensive rese
with real-life examples
unexpected twists and t........ .. ..p,
Making the Leap shows how others have responded to these,
providing ready-made solutions! Each chapter has really helpful reflection points; the questions are invaluable in helping
you apply the experience of others to your own context. In
short, this is a must-read for anyone, at any stage of their
career, who might be considering headship in the future. It
should convince you, in Dr Berry's words, that it is a journey
well worth taking.

Chris Hildrew, Head Teacher, Churchill Academy and Sixth Form

In this tremendously useful book, Jill Berry helps deputy
heads identify the types of unknowns that may be waiting as
deputies move into headship. Wisdom and sage advice can be
found here in abundance. The thought-provoking questions
have already been immensely helpful to me and I know I will
continue to refer to them over the coming months and years.
Dr Berry's findings are rooted in careful research, with reference to many useful first-hand experiences. I would encourage
all those who aspire to headship, or who are newly appointed,
to read this immensely valuable guide.

Clare Sherwood, Head Teacher, The Cathedral School

With her unique and fundamentally joyful, optimistic voice,
Jill shares her impressive wisdom and experience in a book
which is well worth a read, whether you're firmly on the path
to headship or flirting with the idea from a distance. Throughout, she balances impressive wisdom and experience with
humour and humility, challenge with compassion and potential difficult truths with words of comfort. The book is full of

pragmatic advice. The kinds of heads inspired by the Berry school of thought will be the kinds of leaders who give us genuine reason to be optimistic for our children and our students.

Emma Kell, Head of Communications,
Northumberland Park Community School

Dr Jill Berry is a source of inspiration for aspiring and existing school leaders around the country. Here she has shared helpful personal experience, professional insight and imparted pragmatic advice that helped me, as an aspiring head teacher, before, during and after the application process. With Jill's help I now know myself and know the kind of head that I want to be and I am delighted to have found my best fit.

Hannah Wilson, co-founder of #WomenEd,
Head-elect, Aureus School

A must-read for deputies on the journey to headship, those considering making the leap or supporting others to do so. This book offers principled and pragmatic advice that demystifies and makes sense of significant school leadership transition. I have benefited enormously from Jill's wisdom and support in my career and am pleased that she has captured her knowledge and research in such a helpful and accessible way.

Helena Marsh, Executive Principal, Linton Village College

Jill writes for leaders and future leaders everywhere. I love the way that she uses the best research to analyse the journey to headship and beyond. Jill's research conversations with new heads provide useful insights. She reflects on these conversations alongside practical suggestions to help school leaders and – most importantly – poses challenging questions, inspiring us to think deeply for ourselves.

Judith Enright, Head Teacher, Queens Park Community School

Jill's reassuring words of encouragement help you to ask yourself challenging questions – the mark of a great coach – to establish whether headship is right for you and, indeed, whether you are right for headship. Those who decide they are can't help but benefit from her wisdom. Using a perfect balance of personal experience and findings from her doctoral thesis, as well as the best current academic research, Jill is informative and authentic. Her engaging stories, concrete experiences and rhetorical questions are skilfully motivating and inspire you to take the plunge. Jill's words have been a joy to read, giving me the confidence to take my next step. Most importantly she has given me the insight to make this happen. Written for busy people, straight to the point, easy to read and impossible to put down, *Making the Leap* will help any senior leader find the transition to headship a walk in the park!

Kelly Leonard, Assistant Head Teacher, Turton School

I wish I had had the erudite advice of Jill Berry to guide my thinking and help give me some perspective when I was making my decision to apply for headship. Jill's narrative shows enormous empathy and understanding, and reflects absolutely what I was going through during this time in my career transition. The questions for reflection provide just the sort of focus I needed. The experiences and contemplations of Jill and her research participants are without doubt benefitting me as I embark on this crucial next stage in the transition.

Jill's intelligent reflection, advice, recommendations and counsel, all grounded in research as well as extensive experience, have served as an enormous boon to me at a point when I really need it! I would recommend this as a very helpful read to anyone who is even remotely considering the next step in their career.

Ngaire Telford, Head Teacher, Herne Hill School

The most impressive and useful book I have read about preparing for headship and how best to make the transition from deputy to leader of a school: a book of this nature is long overdue. Through interviews with six new heads during their lead-in period Dr Berry has been able to provide insights into the experience of transition to headship as it is lived rather than in retrospect. While well informed by her own academic research, this is nonetheless a highly readable and enjoyable text, with Dr Berry's own experiences and anecdotes placed alongside those of her interviewees. An immensely practical book, I am sure I will be returning to key chapters and sections throughout the coming months and years. The book is very well structured: the key challenges of each stage are first made clear and then addressed with eminently sensible advice. *Making the Leap* is a superb text for giving a sense of the range and variety of the job. For many years to come it will be the text that prospective heads, heads-elect and serving heads take down from their shelves to refer to and reread.

Kevin Carson, Senior Deputy Head, The Grammar School at Leeds

Making the Leap provides insight and understanding into the transition from deputy to head teacher. The book draws not only on Jill's extensive leadership experiences but also those of six deputy head teachers and their leadership journeys. Skilfully written, engaging, thought-provoking and underpinned by high quality academic research: in whatever leadership capacity you are currently working within, there is something in this book for everyone. The book will certainly inspire you to make the leap in leadership.

Stephen T. Logan, Deputy Head Teacher, Malet Lambert School

At last, everyone can access Jill Berry's wisdom, wealth of knowledge and experience. *Making the Leap* is a must-read for any senior leader who aspires to headship. Jill has balanced research from her doctoral findings alongside her own personal career journey to create this incredibly practical, informative, thought-provoking and inspiring book.

The questions for reflection at the end of each chapter are particularly helpful in challenging your own thinking and planning for the next steps in your leadership journey. Jill's passion for education is infectious and I feel humbled to have met her when I was in a middle leadership position. Jill has had a huge impact on my recent career path: now her sound advice and guidance is succinctly transcribed into print form for all to glean from. I will certainly be referring back to the book often as I make the leap!

Shirley Drummond, Head Teacher, St Helen's College

Enjoyable, reassuring and helpful in equal measure, thorough research, fascinating interviews and years of experience mean that Jill's effective strategies and complex ideas are presented to the reader as if they are 'just' common sense. Jill uses all her experience, research and warmth of personality to advise on the emotional aspects of the journey, and also includes excellent, useful practical tips. Jill skilfully explains the role of an effective head in terms of their impact on the school. There is also sage advice for looking after oneself in such a rewarding but challenging role. This book isn't just about how to prepare for becoming, and being, a good head, it's about how to be an effective leader too. The structure is helpful and the questions at the end of each chapter aid reflection and act as action points. It is essential reading for everyone from the ambitious or curious deputy to the head who has been in post for just a year or even beyond. This book will make anyone a better head and, as a result, their school a better school.

Simon Smith, Headmaster, Rydal Penrhos

True to form, Jill has written an extremely thorough and well-researched book, based on her primary research, which involved shadowing six senior leaders over the period from appointment into their first few months as incumbent. Being based on these real, deeply human stories and peppered with Jill's own first-hand experiences, the advice that comes through is authentic and practical. I found Jill's advice on putting together an application and preparing for the interview process hugely useful. Her advice on coping with the disappointment of rejection really made an impression on me: she is searingly honest about her own experiences of failure and how she coped with these. Jill has an upbeat, positive message to all those who have ever tried and failed – with practical advice on how to learn from the experience and bounce back.

A must-read for all those who aspire to headship and want someone who's been there to give them an idea of what it might be like, I finished the book inspired, reassured and determined to continue my bid to become a head teacher.

Dr Tim Jefferis, Deputy Head, Oswestry School

Making the Leap provides an essential guide for all middle and senior leaders who are thinking about, or are about to embark upon, their first headship. It provides clear advice on all the key steps: from considering headship, to the application process, the lead-in period before taking up post and then on how to 'inhabit' the role. Jill bases her advice on her own considerable experience and the research she undertook for her doctoral study. She does not lay out a blueprint for success, rather she considers different approaches and offers sage advice about how different challenges can be faced in a variety of ways. I found the book invaluable – a must-read for all those preparing to take up their first headship. I will be keeping my copy on my desk!

Clare Wagner, Headmistress,
Watford Grammar School for Girls

Dr Jill Berry

Making the leap
Moving from deputy to head

Crown House Publishing Limited
www.crownhouse.co.uk

First published by

Crown House Publishing Ltd
Crown Buildings, Bancyfelin, Carmarthen, Wales, SA33 5ND, UK
www.crownhouse.co.uk

and

Crown House Publishing Company LLC
PO Box 2223, Williston, VT 05495
www.crownhousepublishing.com

First published 2016. Reprinted 2017.

Cover image © losw100, majivecka – fotolia.com, leap graphic © majivecka – fotolia.com

British Library Cataloguing-in-Publication Data
A catalogue entry for this book is available
from the British Library.

Print ISBN 978-178583161-4
Mobi ISBN 978-178583172-0
ePub ISBN 978-178583173-7
ePDF ISBN 978-178583174-4

LCCN 2016953426

Printed and bound in the UK by
TJ International, Padstow, Cornwall

To the memory of Mr R. G. Malyan, with thanks.

Acknowledgements

Thanks to my six research participants who were prepared to give time to supporting my doctoral study at a very busy period in their professional lives, and to my supervisors at the University of Nottingham, Andy Noyes and Andy Townsend.

Thanks are also due to the team at Crown House who have guided me through the publishing process, and to the huge community of educators with whom I interact on Twitter and through the world of blogging from whom I have learnt so much.

Finally, thank you to my mother, Iris Barker, and my husband, John Berry, whose faith in me has been hugely encouraging and motivating in this, as in all my other endeavours.

Contents

Preface: my story

I taught for thirty years between 1980 and 2010, carrying out seven different jobs across six different schools after beginning my teaching career as a secondary English specialist. I loved my time in the classroom (and during my years as a head I continued to teach) but also very much enjoyed the additional challenge of working with and through other staff to reach more students. I was promoted to a pastoral role in my first school (as assistant head of house in a school where the pastoral structure was house based) and then moved to my second school to be second in the English department, then head of English in my third school, head of sixth form in my fourth, deputy head in my fifth and head, for ten years, in my sixth and final school.

I was perhaps fortunate in that I worked in six good schools, alongside some exceptional teachers and support staff and many talented leaders. I also experienced some examples of less effective leadership, but think I learnt even more from these negative role models, and reflecting on how I might lead differently helped me to formulate and refine my vision of the type of leader I one day hoped to be.

The six schools I taught in were all quite different from each other: I worked in the state and independent sectors; in all boys', all girls' and co-educational schools; in comprehensive and selective schools; in 4–18, 7–18 and 11–18 schools. I also taught GCSE and A level to classes of adults in the evenings. I enjoyed my career, particularly headship, which I found joyful, though challenging. However, ten years as a head in one school felt like enough for me, and I had no aspirations to move to a second headship, so at the age of 52 I left full-time teaching/headship and decided to do something different with the final stretch of my professionally useful life.

Having completed a master's degree in education fifteen years into my teaching career, I decided to embark on a professional doctorate in education fifteen years later, and considered that this would constitute an interesting challenge in the 'post-career' phase of my life. It has been said that if you complete a PhD you 'contribute to the body of knowledge of the world', whereas those who opt for a professional doctorate 'contribute to the body of professional knowledge in the world'. The latter appealed to me as I was committed to disseminating anything I learnt to the professional community of which I had been a member for the previous thirty years.

I have always found leadership transitions fascinating. What motivates someone to move from the position of a classroom teacher without specific responsibility to their first middle leadership role? Why do some middle leaders in due course want to make the move to senior leadership? And why do some senior leaders aspire to headship? I realised that I was also going through a further transition: from head teacher to … whatever came next. It caused me to reflect on the challenges and the opportunities of this particular transition.

I knew I wanted to focus on some element of the leadership transition process in my doctoral research project, and opted to home in on the transition from deputy to head. This seemed to me to be the most interesting of leadership transitions, as I considered there was a paradox at the heart of the relationship between deputy headship and headship. On the one hand, being a deputy appears to be the best preparation for headship, offering as it does the opportunity for senior leaders to experience headship 'in miniature': when the head is out of school, the deputy in effect *is* the head. In my case, I knew I wanted to be a head when I realised how much I enjoyed deputising when my head was away. However, in many respects the two roles are quite different. Deputies are far more operational, often preoccupied with the smooth day-to-day running of the school, solving problems and keeping the wheels oiled. Heads, working closely with governors, are far more strategic, involved in the bigger picture, including public relations, representing the school in a range of contexts and engaging with the wider community beyond the school. And, of course, however much autonomy and responsibility a deputy is given, ultimately there is always someone to stand behind – the head to whom they defer. When you become a head, you have to adjust to this new professional persona (which can be a particularly interesting challenge if you are internally appointed to headship). You become 'the one', that figure to whom others defer.

This led me to reflect on what it really means to move from the solution-finding, at times mechanical nuts and bolts, of the deputy role to the one-step-removed head teacher role. What is the nature of this transition? How can aspiring heads, and heads-elect, prepare for it? How can they navigate it so that they begin their headship in as strong a position as possible?

My doctoral research focussed on the challenges of making this transition and the strategies incoming heads use, including the channels of support they access as they face these challenges. In this book I explore my research findings, informed by my wide reading in the field of educational leadership, and underpinned by my experience of making the transition myself and supporting others who are negotiating the process. I hope that what I have to offer is useful to those who are deciding whether headship is the right step for them; to those who are actively aspiring and applying; to heads-elect who are negotiating the lead-in period between being appointed to headship and formally assuming the role; to established heads preparing the next generation of school leaders; to outgoing heads managing their own transition and, I hope, supporting their successors; to governors whose responsibility it is to manage head teacher succession; and to other senior leaders who have an important supporting role to play when the head of the school changes.

It may be that this isn't the kind of book you read from cover to cover, but a book you dip into as different elements become relevant to you: deciding whether to apply for headship, negotiating the application and selection process, making the most of the time immediately following successful appointment and so on. However you choose to use it, I very much hope you will find it helpful as you navigate your leadership journey.

Researchers such as Leithwood et al. (2006) and Barber et al. (2010) have established that school leadership is second only to the quality of teaching in its effect on successful pupil outcomes. Preparing and supporting future generations of incoming head teachers is crucial if schools are to be strong and stable institutions where students and staff thrive. I hope this book has a part to play in this preparation and support of future school leaders.

Chapter 1

Introduction

Making the leap – why would you want to?

Spheres of influence and what is distinctive about headship

It seems to me that when you start teaching, your sphere of influence involves the pupils in the class, or classes, you are timetabled to teach. You focus on their learning in your subject or, if you are a primary teacher, in a range of subjects. You may also build your pastoral skills through your role as a tutor or form teacher, taking greater responsibility for the welfare and well-being of the pupils in your group and, through this, supporting their learning and progress. You care about them as people as well as pupils, and this may also lead to a fuller contribution to the wider life of the school and activities beyond the classroom – for example, through the extra-curricular programme the school offers. Building relationships through such activity can support and strengthen the relationships with those you meet in the classroom. In addition, involvement in the wider life of the school may enable you to establish positive contact with a greater number of children.

For many teachers, the contact with pupils, and the focus on subjects and activities about which they themselves are enthusiastic, and usually talented and knowledgeable, is the appeal of the profession. Being able to communicate the rewards of developing expertise in that subject/area, sharing your passions and enthusing others, is energising and thrilling, though it is also undoubtedly tough, especially if some of those you teach are reluctant to engage and prefer to focus on testing you. However, with increasing experience and growing confidence this can become easier. You learn as they learn – as you continue to practise and hone your craft.

Sometimes you reach the point where you consider yourself ready for further challenge. Inevitably, if you take on greater responsibility, perhaps initially as a middle leader, your teaching is likely to reduce as you are allocated more time for your leadership role. However, my view is that as your sphere of influence expands you begin to affect the lives of more pupils, by working with and through other staff. As a teacher of English my focus was the pupils in my classes. As a second in department and later a head of English my focus was the pupils in all the English lessons, taught by all the English teachers, in the school. I worked with and through other adults to reach more children.

Middle leadership will be a new challenge and will provide you with fresh experiences and opportunities. You realise that encouraging pupils to follow your lead is one thing; encouraging adults to do the same is a challenge of a different order! But leadership can be hugely stimulating and rewarding. How do you earn the trust and respect of those within your domain? How do you win hearts and minds, inspire and encourage? How do you ensure that you get the right balance of support and challenge? It is part of your responsibility to hold the members of your team to account, and not simply to be their indiscriminate advocate who tries to protect and defend them. It takes courage to ensure that, as a team, you all have high aspirations and that any difficult issues are addressed and not ignored. But it is crucial to do this in a positive and supportive way, to lead the team so that everyone has a part to play in its ongoing development: your role is to coordinate the efforts of all the team members, to see the best in others and to be aware of, and make the most of, their complementary strengths. You are not the only one with ideas; you are not necessarily the source of the best ideas; you are not even, necessarily, the best teacher in the team (although you have to be a good, credible teacher). Your job as a leader is to help everyone else to be their best, so that the team grows in strength and effectiveness under your leadership.

There are advantages to having a middle leadership role: often the team you lead has a clearly defined identity with obvious parameters, and it may be of a manageable size. Often teaching and learning are still fundamental to your role, and, for most of us, the things that brought us into the profession in the first place may still be at the core of your day-to-day activity. You can lead change from this position; if the domain for which you are responsible is successful, well led and well respected, you can become a beacon of excellence which demonstrates what can be achieved when the conditions, and the degree of support and challenge, are right. You show convincingly what *can* be done.

However, as a successful middle leader you may feel, in due course, that you would like to have the capacity to make a greater whole-school difference. The leadership skills you are developing, and the achievements you are able to secure within your team, may give you a taste for what you could go on to accomplish with greater responsibility, increased authority and a wider brief. You may, in time, begin to look for a senior leadership position.

Senior leadership posts vary, and if you reach this point in your career it is important to be clear about what kind of area of responsibility appeals to you, and what you believe your temperament, skills and passions best suit you for. What lights your fire? It may be the pastoral element of school life that you find energising and rewarding. It may be the curriculum, timetabling or the leadership of academic teams. It may be a focus on teaching and learning, on professional development, on staff induction and support or on digital learning. It may be the coordination of the extra-curricular elements of the wider school community. Whatever your whole-school role, your sphere of influence will expand. The number of lives you are affecting – both in terms of students' experiences and the full range of teaching and support staff – increases. Your influence on the direction of the school also grows. You can make a bigger difference.

And as a senior leader, especially as a deputy head, you have a taste of how it might be if, in effect, there were no restrictions to your influence, your responsibility and your capacity to direct the school's development. As a head, you will work closely with your governing body, but in many respects you *are* the school – you represent what the school stands for and you take it on the journey you believe to be right for that particular school at that particular stage in its development. This is a huge privilege and a weighty task. But if you have the right temperament, it is, I would suggest, the best job in the world.

So as your career progresses and you move from one leadership role to another, your sphere of influence gradually grows. You will be required to take on new challenges and will, in every new job, be called upon to do things you may never have faced before. You will have the chance to learn, to grow, to prove yourself. You will make mistakes and survive them. But I believe that the qualities that make you a good teacher are closely related to those which will serve you well in leadership. Every teacher is, in fact, a leader of learning within their own classroom. If you decide to move to middle leadership, to senior leadership, to headship ultimately, you will continue to refine these skills, but in my opinion good leaders are good leaders at whatever level.

What makes headship distinctive? It is undoubtedly a big job. You need a clear grasp of the big picture – what the school stands for and where it is going – because no school stands still. During the course of a working week you may experience a huge range of different tasks: a governors' meeting debating future strategy; a finance meeting looking at budgetary priorities and constraints; leading an assembly; interviewing staff; meeting parents. You might be working within the community as a representative of the school you lead and a spokesperson for education. You will certainly spend considerable time with your senior leadership team, making the most of their complementary skills and ensuring that, in the words of Dylan Wiliam, they work 'as a team' rather than simply 'in a team'. Heads do not have to be able to do everything themselves; in fact, it is unrealistic to expect them to be good at everything. However, they do need to ensure that all the bases are covered. They need to be self-aware and to recognise when they are drawing on the expertise of others. They need to know the questions to ask and to be able to understand the answers, to probe where necessary and to have a secure overview of all aspects of the running of the school. If things go wrong, they are, together with the governing body, responsible. But developing and making the most of the skills of all members of the school community is a crucial part of the way in which successful heads operate. They lift and inspire, they encourage and motivate. They lead.

There are a number of ways in which those who aspire to headship can prepare themselves to take on this ultimate responsibility for school leadership, and these ways will be explored in subsequent chapters. They need to develop a clear conception of what the best school leadership looks like, where their own strengths are and in which areas they are still learning and strengthening their capabilities. They will have been formulating their vision of the kind of head they might one day hope to be throughout their careers, even through their own schooldays. They will have learnt both from positive examples and also from negative role models, who may have taught them about the pitfalls they hope to avoid. However, there is much about headship for which it is difficult, perhaps even impossible, to prepare yourself. All heads will face unexpected challenges which will test them in ways they have not been able to anticipate. When they face such challenges they will need to be adaptable, quick-thinking and keen to learn. They will need to understand where they can go for support and counsel, but they will also need the courage to make what may be difficult decisions and to show real leadership in the times when they, and perhaps the school, are tested.

Robert Quinn (2004: 153) talks of how as a leader you need the 'adaptive confidence to walk naked into the land of uncertainty and to build the bridge as you walk on it'. No beginning head is the finished article. It could be argued that this is a stage which no head ever reaches, as we are constantly learning and evolving. Certainly, more than five years since I finished my own headship I feel I am still learning about school leadership – from my reading and research, from my reflections after a thirty-year career, from contact with others in my consultancy work and also from my engagement with educational professionals through social networking. Aspiring heads need to have sufficient self-belief to recognise that much of being a head they will learn from the experience of being a head.

In the following chapters I focus specifically on the process of transition, and what it means to relinquish the professional persona of a senior leader and to take on the professional identity of the head teacher. It is a journey which is well worth taking.

Questions for reflection

■ Can you describe your current professional sphere of influence?

■ How might this sphere of influence expand were you to move into a new professional role?

- What is the appeal of this potentially extended sphere of influence? What do you anticipate it would enable you to do, and why might this be an attractive proposition for you?

- What challenges might this greater sphere of influence bring?

- Consider how you can best prepare yourself to face the challenges, and to make the most of the opportunities, presented by this extension to your sphere of influence.

My own experience

I started considering headship applications in the third year of my time as a deputy. I very much enjoyed being a deputy head, but when my head was out of school and people looked to me in her place, I found this was an opportunity I relished rather than shrank from. My deputy headship had helped me to clarify my thinking about the type of school I wanted to lead – the environment in which I felt I could be the kind of school leader I hoped to be, and where my temperament and skills might perhaps be best suited. So in year three I started to look at the vacancies that were out there and began to apply.

I had four headship interviews in years three and four of my deputy headship, and was successful at the fourth attempt. The selection process took place late in the summer term, with the appointment beginning at the start of the autumn term the following year, so I had just over a year's lead-in time. I found this invaluable; in that year I attended a number of events in my new school, just to watch, listen and learn. I discovered more about 'how it is done here': the parent–teacher association annual general meeting, the award of A level prizes and certificates, a music concert in partnership with other schools in the grand Birmingham Symphony Hall, the opening of a new building. It was excellent to have the time and space for reflection. What was the school clearly strong at? Where was it continuing to develop? Where might I be able to find, or create, the space to make my own contribution, and to put my stamp on the role and the school? This was a school which had already existed for 118 years before I arrived as its eighth head teacher.

It is perhaps interesting how difficult it can be to appreciate how typical our own experience is, as we often have no clear frame of reference and nothing to compare it with. It was over a decade after making the transition to headship myself that I conducted my professional doctorate in education research into the experiences of six other deputies moving to their first headship, in each case involving a change of school. Reflecting on their experiences, and what appeared to be distinctive about the nature of transition, made me appreciate that in a number of ways I was particularly fortunate – something I did not necessarily realise at the time. I'm now grateful for the following factors/elements:

- My predecessor was positive and supportive, and clearly invested in helping me to make a success of the transition. She was comfortable with her own decision to leave; she was retiring after ten years as head of the school which had followed on from a first headship elsewhere. She did everything she could to ensure the lead-in period was a productive experience for me and for those with whom I would be working as head. She understood that the focus should be on what was good for the school, not on herself. She had invested ten years in making the school stronger than she had found it. She wanted me to build on that and to make a success of leading the school. This, of course, should be the norm. It was over a decade later that I discovered that this was not necessarily always the case.

- The head in the school where I was a deputy was proud of my success in securing a headship of my own; she was pleased for me and never at any stage grudging about the potential for divided loyalties as I fulfilled a demanding deputy head role while beginning to plan and prepare for taking on my headship. She allowed me time out of school when I needed it. She was keen to share with me the demands and opportunities of her own role to help me see ever more clearly what the role of head might require from me. She expressed sadness at the fact that I would be moving on – she and I had worked very well together – while balancing this with the firm sense that she felt I would be a good head and that headship would be an experience I would relish and find fulfilling. She never made me feel guilty about leaving the school in order to develop my own career.

- The chair of governors, along with the governing body and members of the overarching trust of which the school I was joining was a member, was quick to express confidence in me, reassuring me that my appointment was a unanimous decision and that he had faith in my capacity to step up to the role. Although I was fifteen years younger than the outgoing head and had no experience of headship, as my predecessor had had on her appointment, I never felt that there was any nervousness on the part of the governing body that I might not be up to the task.

- The school community I got to know during the year-long lead-in period were warm and welcoming, and during this time I was able to build positive relationships with senior leaders, other teaching and support staff, members of the overarching trust, some parents and some students. I was not overwhelmed with requests to take on tasks or to make decisions which would have been difficult for a head-elect who was fulfilling a demanding role some distance away, and who did not yet have the knowledge base to make such decisions. I never felt I was being 'grilled' about my vision for the school and how it might develop under my leadership. I was never pressured if invited to events I was unable to attend because of clashing commitments at the school where I was currently employed. However, I was sufficiently involved in the life of the school to which I was moving to feel that I was building my knowledge and familiarity with its ethos, its systems and with the people who made it work so well. I was starting to know, and also starting to be known.

In retrospect, this new school community coped better with the change of head than it might have done – losing a well-established, well-respected and experienced head and inheriting in her place an untried deputy. However,

I believe that the carefully considered and well-planned use of the lead-in period was largely responsible for the smoothness of the transition.

When I left the headship ten years later, I ensured that I resigned sufficiently early to allow the school to appoint my successor a year in advance of her taking up the appointment. I knew, liked and respected the head they chose to succeed me, and was heartened by the choice the selection panel had made. I did everything I could to ensure that she felt welcomed into the school and positively supported as she prepared to make the transition. She and I continue to have a very good relationship five years later. As my predecessor had done, I could see that the ongoing success of the school was paramount, and helping the incoming head to make a success of her headship was the last thing I could do to secure its positive future.

Questions for reflection

■ If you are an aspiring head or a head-elect, what experiences in your career thus far have helped to prepare you for making the transition to headship?

■ Stop for a moment and consider the positives: what do you have to be grateful for in terms of the support you have received up to this point?

■ Now consider the challenges: how will you navigate these challenges so they do not have a damaging effect on the process of transition to headship?

■ Consider your motivation for headship: what would you say are the main drivers, as far as you are concerned?

My research

I began my professional doctorate in education studies in the autumn of 2010, having left headship that summer. I was interested in further study and keen to continue learning and ensure I was stretched and challenged intellectually. I followed a taught course for two years, part-time, where we covered concepts such as the theory of knowledge, different methodologies and research ethics. I planned and conducted my own research in years three and four, and completed the analysis and writing of the thesis in year five, submitting at the beginning of year six.

I knew from the outset that I wished to focus on educational leadership. I decided part way through the first year that I might want to concentrate on making the transition to headship. I was particularly interested, not just in new headship, but in the process of moving from being a deputy head to being the head, and what this meant in terms of role identity. It seemed to me that this was a complex process because, although being a deputy gave you a taste of headship, it was in many respects a very different job. Moving from this role to the head's role involved, to some degree, professionally reinventing yourself, while still ensuring you remained true to your core values and did not distort who you were and what you believed in.

Early in the taught course I completed an assignment in which I analysed fifteen different academic articles about making the move from deputy to head, conducting a critical review of what I had learnt from them about the process. (The fifteen papers which covered the transition to headship in a range of countries are listed at the end of this chapter.) I considered both what the main challenges of making the transition were and what support strategies were available to those going through the process. From my analysis of the articles, I concluded that the main challenges related to:

- The process of socialisation as the incoming head adapted to their new professional persona. The experience of moving to headship changed them in some ways, and they changed the school they joined by enacting the role differently from their predecessor.

- Coping with change (both the change in themselves and their role) and coping with managing change as they moved into headship. However strong the school they were joining appeared to be, there would be ways in which they would wish to lead it differently, and in so doing make their mark and put their stamp on both the school and their role within it. This would involve ensuring that the pace of any change introduced was neither too rapid nor too slow.

- Dealing with pressure. Pressure comes from a variety of sources and it builds from the time of the appointment, even before the new head officially assumes the role. Some of it stems from the incoming head's expectations of themselves. Building resilience in the face of this pressure is a challenge.

- Building relationships. Again, this process begins from the time of the selection and successful appointment. There are many individuals and groups both within and beyond the school with whom an incoming head needs to establish positive relationships, and this includes the outgoing head in addition to governors, the whole range of staff, pupils, parents and members of the wider community outside the school gates.

- Survival in the light of all the above. These newly appointed heads are already carrying out a demanding and time-consuming job in their current schools. Increasingly, they feel pulled towards the new role and the challenges and opportunities they will face there. Balancing the two competing sets of demands is taxing and requires significant skill and a clear focus on different priorities at different times. Throughout all this the head-elect has to be able to look after themselves, ensuring they have the reserves of energy they need and a healthy and sustainable balance in their lives.

My analysis of the articles I had selected also suggested a number of ways in which these fledgling heads could be supported through the process of transition as they faced such challenges. In some cases they were drawing on their own resources and devising their own strategies; at other times they were accessing external sources of support. The main strategies and sources of support they mobilised included the following:

- Formal preparation programmes. Those who had made the conscious decision that they wanted to progress to headship in due course often undertook specific training to prepare themselves for making the move. In the UK this included the National Professional Qualification for Headship (NPQH), at that time still mandatory for maintained sector head teachers in this country. Other aspiring heads opted for master's degrees or short courses focussing on the particular elements of headship that they might not have had extensive experience of in their deputy role – for example, overall financial management of the school, closer working relationships with governors, and legal and regulatory issues.

- Prior experience. The aspiring head teachers in the studies could see how they had been honing their craft and building their leadership capacity throughout their careers, and even before they joined the teaching profession. Some had experience beyond teaching which contributed to the development of relevant skills, including in some cases what they had discovered as parents. They learnt particularly from the heads they had supported as senior leaders, some of whom had been strongly invested in the personal and professional development of deputy heads who they saw might eventually proceed to headship.

- Key mentors and influencers included such heads, but went beyond this to include significant figures in these aspiring heads' professional and personal lives who had guided, supported, counselled and inspired them. Sometimes these figures were within the schools where the heads-elect were fulfilling their deputy role; sometimes they were from earlier schools in which these new heads had taught; sometimes they were outside the world of education. Building relationships and alliances with those in the school they were to join as heads, including the governors, was also relevant.

- Finally, learning from feedback was a significant source of support. The incoming heads ideally needed to be receptive and responsive, prepared to listen and strongly disposed to learn. This was a key feature of the lead-in period between being appointed to the role and officially assuming it. It included learning from and benefiting from the wisdom, experience and expertise of the head they were succeeding, provided that the dynamic between them was sufficiently positive for this predecessor to be a useful source of support as these deputies prepared to make the move to their first headship.

One of the interesting findings from my analysis concerned the issue of context. On the one hand, an understanding of context appeared to be crucial to the success of an incoming head. Every school is different, and a new head has to take the temperature and tune in to the needs and priorities of the school they are to lead at this particular point in its journey. Indeed, one of the issues of second or subsequent headships is that they can fail (even when the school leader's first headship was a success) if the new incumbent does not take into account the context of the school they are now joining sufficiently carefully. However, from considering the range of studies it became apparent that the challenges of new headship are not necessarily context-dependent. So, dealing with the issues of socialisation into a new professional identity, coping with change and pressure, building relationships and finding balance were issues for incoming heads whatever the situation they were stepping into. These challenges crossed geographical boundaries (and so were relevant to leadership of schools in different countries), different education systems and sectors (for example, those with or without mandatory preparation programmes for heads, or across maintained and independent schools) and different time frames. Weindling and Dimmock (2006), for instance, draw on research into the transition to headship conducted by Earley and Weindling from the 1980s onwards. The challenges faced by those new to headship over thirty years ago were not significantly different from those experienced by deputies moving into headship today.

Completing this assignment and learning from the research and reflections of others on the subject of transition to headship whetted my appetite and confirmed my commitment to conducting my own research which would enable me to look in more detail at the specific experiences of individuals at this particular stage in their career. I was keen to find out more, to see what I could learn which would contribute to the field and add to the store of what was already known about the challenges of transition and the support available to those facing these challenges. In the third year of my part-time doctoral studies I therefore designed a research project of my own.

I contacted several head teacher associations with which I had a prior relationship from my own time as a head and, through these gatekeepers, identified a number of serving deputies who had already been appointed to headships beginning in the autumn term 2013. From this group I found six participants who were willing to work with me on my research project. I explained that my intention was to visit each of them three times, to conduct a semi-structured interview on each occasion and also to shadow them as they went about their jobs. At stages one and two they would still be deputies, and I would therefore be interviewing them and shadowing them while they fulfilled their deputy role and planned for the future. At stage three I would visit them in the school where they had assumed their headship, interview them and observe them as they carried out their role as a new head teacher. One of the advantages of my research design was the immediacy and dynamism of charting the transition to headship as it was actually being lived, rather than asking participants to recall the experience retrospectively. In this respect my study differed from many of those I had so far considered in my doctoral reading.

A semi-structured interview has a degree of flexibility built into it: generally the interviewer uses a written guide to ensure that they cover a similar range of areas with each participant, but it is not rigidly organised, leaving scope for the interviewees to direct the course of the conversation to some extent, and in this way to focus on and talk about elements of their experience which they believe to be significant but which the interviewer may not have anticipated. Before each interview I shared the written guide with the participants, reasoning that, were I in their position, I would wish to prepare myself mentally for the questions and discussion with the researcher at each stage.

Observation or shadowing was a strategy which would enable me to gauge what these participants said within the context of what they did, to watch them in action and to see how others responded to them. It would also allow me to reflect on any differences between how they behaved as a deputy and how they conducted themselves as a head. Over the course of my eighteen visits, three visits to each of my six participants, I observed them teach; address groups of pupils, staff and parents; chair meetings of different types; take assembly; and meet individual members of staff and students for a variety of reasons. I saw them formally on duty and in informal contact with pupils, staff, parents and other visitors as they moved around the school at breaktimes and lunchtimes. I even watched one participant manage an unanticipated fire evacuation of the whole school. The range of activities I observed was helpful in giving me insight into the varied, and at times disjointed, responsibilities of my participants as both deputy and head. It also helped me to consider any ways in which I felt my participants were changing over time, and how they were socialising into their new professional identity.

In addition to the semi-structured interviews and the shadowing/observation, I also decided to conduct what Bush (2009) calls 'role-set analysis'. An individual's role-set involves all those within their sphere of influence, so, in the case of head teachers, those whose professional lives are affected by the way in which the head carries out their job. By interviewing, informally, representatives of this role-set I was afforded an additional, wider perspective on how these incoming heads were managing the transition. So, in the schools where they were carrying out their deputy role while managing the lead-in period before they moved to headship, I spoke to their current head teacher, their personal assistant (PA) if they had one, other senior staff, a range of teaching and support staff and pupils. Once they had moved to headship and I visited them in their new school, I met and discussed how they were perceived to be managing their move into headship with the chair of governors who had led the panel which appointed them, with their PAs, members of the senior leadership team including the bursar/business manager, groups of teaching and support staff including middle leaders, groups of pupils and, in some cases, parents. I also spoke to my participants' wives and husbands where this was possible. All six participants were moving to a different part of the country, uprooting their families in addition to embarking on a new professional challenge themselves. So wives and husbands were leaving jobs or changing jobs; children were leaving their friends and establishing themselves in new schools; all of these families were settling into new homes. All of the beginning heads in my study were aware of the weight of personal responsibility this placed upon them, in addition to the increased professional responsibility they were about to embrace.

I had deliberately chosen six new heads who were all moving schools. It seemed to me that managing the transition to headship when internally promoted brings a particular range of challenges (in addition to some advantages), and I wanted all of my participants to be on the same page as far as moving into a new community and establishing themselves as the head there was concerned. In subsequent chapters I shall address the issue of making the transition to headship in the school where you are currently serving as deputy, but for the benefit of my own research I discounted potential participants who were internally promoted. I also discounted from inclusion in my sample any heads-elect who were currently fulfilling a role other than a senior deputy head who had had the opportunity to deputise for their current head when that head was out of school. I wanted them all to have had the taste of ultimate school leadership which this allows. This deputising responsibility had motivated them to apply for headship, rather than deterred them from it.

However, across the six participants accepted into the study there were a range of individuals and schools represented. There were three men and three women. One was a primary head and five secondary – as my own background was as a secondary specialist I wanted to focus on the experience of leading a senior school or an all-age school, as I had done. The schools covered single sex and co-educational schools; small, medium and large schools; day schools and schools with a boarding element. They were also located all over England. The stage was set!

I visited my six participants for the first time around Easter 2013 in the schools where they were deputies. Some of them had only recently been appointed to their headships; others had already experienced one or two terms of the lead-in period since being successful at interview. On this occasion we focussed on their journey to headship – their motivation for applying, their experience of the appointment process (in two cases they had achieved success in their first application; the remaining four had applied for a number of headships before reaching this point). We explored how it felt to have been successful, including how the news had been received in their current school and whether they felt any differently in their deputy role since their headship appointment had been confirmed. We also discussed their experiences of the lead-in period so far, and how they were planning on using the summer term and the summer holiday before officially stepping into the role at the beginning of September.

My second visit took place towards the end of the summer term 2013, just before these six deputies moved on from their current schools. The focus on this occasion was how the lead-in period had developed and how well prepared they felt they were for the next stage of their career. We talked about what strategies they had adopted to help them deal with getting the balance right – still committing to their deputy role and current school and not seeming to lack conviction or loyalty, while also increasingly thinking about and preparing for their next role. In some cases, the participants felt the school to which they were moving, and the incumbent head there, had kept them at arm's length and had not been particularly welcoming or keen to involve them. One of the heads-elect found her predecessor head actively hostile. In other cases the heads-elect felt they were being contacted too frequently and asked to involve themselves in, and to make decisions about, issues they did not yet feel well placed to address. Such dilemmas will be addressed more fully in Chapter 3 on managing the lead-in period.

At the stage two interviews I also discussed with my participants what they were anticipating might be the early challenges they would face once they stepped into the headship, and how what they had learnt during the lead-in period had clarified their thinking about and confirmed their perceptions of such challenges. The issue of legacy was key: what they were inheriting from their predecessors had a significant impact on my participants' experience of the transition through the lead-in period and into their early months in post. We then discussed the strategies and channels of support they expected they would be able to access, including the networks they were already working to construct, as they addressed these challenges. One particularly significant network was the group of fellow new heads which some of them had been introduced to through the heads' associations' formal new heads' induction programmes they had undergone.

The third and final visits to my participants took place in January 2014, when they had experienced their first term as a head and then had the Christmas break to reflect and draw breath. With respect to the issue of reflection, all six commented on how being involved in the research process had encouraged them to carve out time to consider their experience of transition in a more structured and formal way than they might otherwise have done: how they believed things were going, how they were feeling and what they were learning. It is perhaps too easy, when we are doing a busy job, to be overwhelmed by what Maggie Farrar, then acting chief executive at the National College, called 'the tyranny of stuff' (see Bannister, 2013), and not to give sufficient thought to how we can perhaps be more effective in the role.

At stage three our focus was on comparing what had been anticipated and what had actually been experienced. What were the unexpected challenges, how had they been addressed and what had been learnt from them that might strengthen these new heads in the future? Where were the shocks and surprises? Where were the early satisfactions and pleasures? What did they think of it so far?

All of my participants recognised that, although there are a number of ways in which you can prepare to take up your headship (and all *had* prepared to some degree), there are some elements of school leadership for which you cannot plan. Three of them, for example, had unfortunately had to deal with bereavement within the school community. Others had found resistance in both expected and unexpected quarters. Four of my participants had members within their senior leadership teams who had applied for the headship and been unsuccessful, and managing these colleagues' disappointment and still building a mutually trusting and positive relationship was not always straightforward. Some had discovered that their assumptions of how a head should carry out the role conflicted with the expectations of different members or groups within the school community. All had preconceptions, perhaps based on their own experience of headship in other schools, in combination with their own sense of moral purpose. The school communities they joined harboured preconceptions of their own, sometimes based on the norms of headship behaviour established by their predecessors (and in some cases by the heads that preceded them). There was therefore the need for some compromise and recalibration, generally on both sides. The process of socialisation was reciprocal – my participants were changing the school in subtle ways as they stepped into the head's role, but they were also, themselves, being changed. This was a nuanced and incremental process.

It was interesting to observe how dealing with unexpected challenges had tested these new heads, while at the same time it had offered them an invaluable opportunity to show their mettle, and thus to prove themselves – both to themselves and to others. In tackling a demanding issue – a difficult safeguarding case, staff disciplinary cases or unexpectedly poor GCSE results, for example – these incoming heads created a space within which they could demonstrate their strength. They therefore emerged from the challenge in a more secure position than they were in before the demanding situation arose.

Throughout all three stages of the research project, I discussed with my participants, and with the members of the role-set, what particular strategies and sources of support were proving to be of benefit as they faced the different challenges that making the transition to headship presented to them. All participants talked of role models and mentors who had inspired and encouraged them in the past, and in many cases continued to do so. The head in the school where they were a deputy was a particularly significant figure, and the most supportive of these had invested time and energy in helping to prepare their deputy to step up to headship from the time when they were first appointed to the senior leadership team. Their experience, especially as deputies, was key, and several remarked on how they recognised that the range of issues they had dealt with as deputies had helped them to build the skills and the confidence they now needed to draw on as heads.

During the lead-in period, these heads-elect were generally astute in identifying possible gaps in their expertise and confidence, and using staff in their current schools, and former colleagues and friends in other schools, to help them to build their knowledge and skills about, for example, the Early Years Foundation Stage, finance, governance and marketing.

New heads' induction courses facilitated the creation of a network of their peers, all at a similar stage on their professional journey, to whom they could turn if they needed advice or just a listening ear; some felt that no one quite understood their perspective like fellow new heads who were going through the same transition process.

Many talked of the support of friends and family who kept them grounded, and partners who encouraged them to 'switch off' (sometimes literally, insisting they disconnect from the devices which linked them to school concerns and personnel), to stop them neglecting the personal/professional balance which was key to their well-being and to ensuring they paced themselves in a way which was healthy and sustainable.

My participants were also aware of relying on their own resources, finding inner strength and resilience from their own sense of a moral code and their clear vision and values. This sustained them in difficult times when they faced the more demanding initial challenges.

From my semi-structured interviews with these new heads, from shadowing/observing them as they went about their jobs and seeing them in action, and from talking to others about their perceptions of how the participants were managing their transition into the role, a number of key findings emerged. The different elements of these findings will be explored in subsequent chapters, so that the experiences of my six participants may inform, and ideally benefit, future generations of aspiring and new heads.

The key message to emerge from the research was this: making the transition to first-time headship is a process which involves negotiating the tensions, and finding balance, between inheriting the role from your predecessor and inhabiting the role and making it your own. Throughout this process, both the incoming head and the members of the school community they join are socialised into a new role and a new relationship, as the new head and the new school influence, and are influenced by, each other.

Beneath this overarching message sit three sub-findings:

1. The lead-in period between being appointed and formally taking up the role offers crucial opportunities to begin to tune in to the new school context, to start to know and to be known. It is a challenging time as the head-elect prepares to leave well (handing over their deputy head responsibilities and readying the school for their departure) while at the same time plans to begin well in their new role, preparing the school for their arrival.

2. The relationship which develops between outgoing and incoming head has a significant impact on the process of transition and the new head's capacity to establish themselves during the lead-in period and in the early months in post. Although incoming heads have to negotiate this relationship, they are not fully able to control it. In addition, the legacy the outgoing head leaves behind presents both challenges and opportunities to their successor.

3. There are a number of ways in which heads-elect can prepare to take up the role of school leader, but they ultimately learn how to be a head from being a head. Because of the reciprocal socialisation process the incoming head and the school community they join undergo, the school leader role and the dynamic between leader and led continue to evolve. The incoming heads may prepare as thoroughly as they can, yet it is impossible for them fully to anticipate how it will be once they take up the role. Although they have observed how their new school operates from the vantage point of the lead-in period, the context changes when they are in post and become

part of that landscape. They will meet early unexpected challenges which will test them, including those which arise from reciprocal socialisation, but such challenges also give them the opportunity to prove themselves and to make their mark.

In the following chapters I offer advice to aspiring heads and heads-elect on how to approach (and ideally succeed in) the application and selection process; how to manage the lead-in period between being successfully appointed and formally assuming the role, including achieving a manageable and sustainable balance as you fulfil a demanding job while preparing to assume your headship; how to establish yourself in the early months in post; and how to build on this as you move from being 'the new head' to simply 'the head'. I also consider what might come after your first headship. Throughout the book I draw on my own experience, my wide reading, what I have learnt from my leadership consultancy work and also, crucially, from the experiences of my six research participants.

Gronn (1999: xiii) claims: 'The time is well overdue for the field to take seriously the documented experiences of people as they go about acquiring a sense of themselves as leaders and to pass on the benefits of those insights to those coming up behind them.' My research, reported here for a professional audience rather than an academic one, is my attempt to communicate what can be learnt from the experiences of deputies as they make the transition to their first headship. There are lessons here not just for aspiring heads, heads-elect and new heads, but also for the governors who appoint them, for fellow members of the senior leadership team who have a significant part to play in supporting both outgoing and incoming heads, and for established heads who may be investing in the professional development of their own senior leaders and, in due course, preparing to move on from headship themselves.

Questions for reflection

■ Is there anything emerging from my research which initially surprises you?

■ Is there anything which connects with your own experience of what happens in a school when the head changes?

■ If you are an aspiring head, which elements of managing the transition would you expect to find the most challenging?

■ If you are a head-elect, which strategies and sources of support do you believe you could perhaps make more of and benefit from?

References

Browne-Ferrigno, T. (2003) Becoming a principal: role conceptions, initial socialization, role-identity transformation, purposeful engagement, *Educational Administration Quarterly* 39(4): 468–503.

Cheung, R. M. and Walker, A. (2006) Inner worlds and outer limits: the formation of beginning school principals in Hong Kong, *Journal of Educational Administration* 44(4): 389–407.

Cowie, M. and Crawford, M. (2009) Headteacher preparation programmes in England and Scotland: do they make a difference to the first-year head? *School Leadership and Management* 29(1): 5–21.

Crow, G. (2006) Complexity and the beginning principal in the United States: perspectives on socialization, *Journal of Educational Administration* 44(4): 310–325.

Crow, G. (2007) The professional and organizational socialization of new English head teachers in school reform contexts, *Educational Management Administration and Leadership* 35(1): 51–72.

Daresh, J. and Male, T. (2000) Crossing the border into leadership: experiences of newly appointed British head teachers and American principals, *Educational Management and Administration* 28(1): 89–101.

Draper, J. and McMichael, P. (1998) Making sense of primary headship: the surprises awaiting new heads, *School Leadership and Management* 18(2): 197–211.

Hobson, A., Brown, K., Ashy, P., Keys, W., Sharp, C. and Benefield, P. (2003) *Issues for Early Headship – Problems and Support Strategies.* Nottingham: NCSL.

Kelly, A. and Saunders, N. (2010) New heads on the block: three case studies of transition to primary school headship, *School Leadership and Management* 30(2): 127–142.

Quong, T. (2006) Asking the hard questions: being a beginning principal in Australia, *Journal of Educational Administration* 44(4): 376–388.

Sackney, L. and Walker, K. (2006) Canadian perspectives on beginning principals: their role in building capacity for learning communities, *Journal of Educational Administration* 44(4): 341–358.

Sarros, A. and Sarros, J. (2007) The first 100 days: leadership challenges of a new CEO, *Educational Management Administration and Leadership* 35(3): 349–371.

Stevenson, H. (2006) Moving towards, into and through principalship: developing a framework for researching the career trajectories of school leaders, *Journal of Educational Administration* 44(4): 408–420.

Walker, A. and Qian, H. (2006) Beginning principals: balancing at the top of the greasy pole, *Journal of Educational Administration* 44(4): 297–309.

Weindling, D. and Dimmock, C. (2006) Sitting in the 'hot seat': new head teachers in the UK, *Journal of Educational Administration* 44(4): 326–340.

Chapter 2

Applying for headship

Key principles of making a successful application

Deciding what to apply for

The previous chapter, and the issue of how your sphere of influence expands as you move up through the different levels of leadership in a school, tells us something about what motivates teachers to begin to move out of the classroom and into different leadership and management roles. Although teaching may continue to be an important part of what such leaders do every day (and even as a head you can choose to teach if that is what you decide to do), the time allocated to teaching inevitably reduces as leadership responsibilities grow. The trade-off for this reduced time spent on enthusing young people about your particular subject area(s) is that you have a greater opportunity to enthuse other adults about teaching and learning and the care of pupils, and to ensure these are as successful as possible. Working with and through other staff enables you to make a greater difference to the lives of more pupils, and at the same time you begin to have a greater impact on the lives of these adults too.

However, what motivates us to take on leadership roles in school settings may not be dramatically different from what brought us into teaching in the first place. When working with trainee teachers (something I do as part of my educational consultancy work) and asking them what led to their commitment to join the profession, the idea of 'making a difference' looms large. They express the conviction that education is a life-changer, a way in which young people can start to take control and ensure they have a range of options which will bring them satisfaction and a sense of achievement. This is a process they are keen to contribute to and support.

Similarly, when I work with aspiring middle leaders, senior leaders and heads, I encourage them to 'start with the why', as Simon Sinek (2009) says. Why do they want to move to this particular role? What do they believe the new level of responsibility will enable them to achieve, and how will that be more rewarding and fulfilling than their current role? What is appealing about the expanded sphere of influence accorded by the position to which they aspire? How do they intend to capitalise on this to be even more effective in the future? And are they looking beyond that to future levels? Do ambitious middle leaders preparing for senior leadership have their sights ultimately set on headship, and is becoming a senior leader seen as a stepping stone along the way?

Of my six research participants, three told me they had always planned to become heads one day, even from the time they entered the teaching profession. The other three said that, for them, the focus was on doing each job they had to the best of their ability until they reached a natural point where they felt ready for a new challenge. The idea of facing such a challenge, testing and proving themselves, is part of the appeal for some. Undoubtedly, gaining promotion, increased status, a higher salary and so having the capacity to provide a better quality of life for themselves and their families will also be a motivating factor for others. But, in my experience, the idea of making a difference to the lives of young people is always there as a driving force when educators consider the reasons behind their desire for career progression. Aspiring heads often see the focus on strategy, vision and values as a key way in which they can achieve this.

It is important that aspiring heads are able to articulate in a clear and compelling way why headship appeals, why they consider they are ready for it, and what they have learnt, experienced and achieved which could contribute to their successful fulfilment of the role. But the other key question to consider is: why would you want to be the head of this particular school at this particular point in its history?

In Chapter 1 I described the importance of context. Although the challenges involved in the process of moving from deputy to head may not be context-dependent, nevertheless sensitivity to context appears to be a crucial element in making a success of school leadership. Incoming heads have to be able to demonstrate their growing knowledge and developing understanding of the needs of the specific school they are joining, and show an assurance that they can adapt to these needs and be the leader the school requires at this time. There has been considerable research into different leadership styles in recent decades – for example, the work of the Hay Group (www.haygroup. com) who have produced an inventory of leadership styles (coercive, authoritative, affiliative, democratic, pace-setting and coaching).

However, there is a general recognition in the research literature that leaders need to be flexible, to have a range of different techniques and strategies in their leadership toolkit and to draw on the appropriate style at the required time. Knowing what the school needs from its leader and how best to move towards desired outcomes is a key part of being an effective head.

During the course of our careers we develop a sense of the kind of head we would one day hope to be. We will have learnt about leadership, and our capacity to lead, from experiences as a member of teams led by others and from our time as a middle and senior leader. In my opinion, being a head is not dramatically different in nature from being an effective head of department, the leader of a pastoral team or a deputy head. Leadership is both simple and complex: it is simply about getting the best from all the individuals within the teams for which you are responsible, so that the whole is greater than the sum of its parts. Leadership is also complex because *how* you do that can be taxing. Can you see the best in each member of your team? Can they see you see it? Do you recognise their skills and strengths (some may not be immediately apparent) and their potential? Can you offer each individual the right balance of support and challenge? In addition to the fact that different individuals require a different balance from others, a specific member of staff may also need the balance to be recalibrated at different times, depending on their growing confidence, or ebbing confidence, personal circumstances or state of health. Do you have the capability to recognise this and to adapt accordingly? If you can manage this successfully at middle or senior leader level, that augurs well for your capacity to do so as a head. The nature of leadership will not dramatically alter. The scale/scope of your leadership influence, however, will.

So when considering headship applications, sensitivity to context and an awareness of your own skills, strengths and preferences should help you to decide which particular headship roles might be best suited to you and which specific vacancies might be appropriate, because you have the ability to provide what this school needs at this time. You will grow into the role, learn from experience and develop your skills and capabilities over time, but from the outset you need to consider that you and the school/role are a good fit.

As an incoming head you inherit a great deal. You inherit an existing ethos and culture – for example, a set of values and a vision and the core behaviours which underpin this. No school's vision and values are set in stone and immutable; vision evolves and develops over time. However, as an incoming head you need to feel comfortable that the vision and values you inherit are ones you can live with and build on. If you believe the school currently stands for something which is alien to your educational philosophy and principles, I would suggest this is not the right context for you.

Clearly, over time, you will have formulated and clarified what your educational philosophy and principles are, and you will articulate them in your application and at interview. You will be appointed to a headship partly on the strength of them; an astute selection panel should be able to identify that you are a good match for where the school currently is and what it needs going forward. However, you will not import your own vision and values; you will work with the school community to support it to develop, articulate, communicate and then 'live' its own, to which you will make a strong contribution. If you are to do so successfully, your starting point needs to be a connection between what you stand for as an educationalist, where the school is now and where it is heading.

Similarly, an incoming head inherits a governing body (although this, too, may well change and develop during the time of your tenure), a senior leadership team (which may include unsuccessful headship candidates), a staff body, a parent body, a student body and an established position within the wider community. The school will have a reputation locally (even nationally or internationally in the case of some very well-known schools) and this is something you will initially have to work with.

My strong advice is that when you begin to apply for headships you do so with careful thought and discrimination. Do your research, read widely and think deeply. Know yourself, and know the context of the vacancies you are considering. Is this a good match? If so, the application and selection process will test your capacity to demonstrate that, not only are you a fit to the school/role, but you are the *best* fit in the field of candidates they are considering. However, if you are not a good match, for whatever reason, I would advise against applying simply for the experience and hoping that the selection panel is astute enough not to appoint you to a school and a position which is patently not the right one for you – because you are not the right head for them. Not getting a job is not the worst scenario. Somehow managing to secure a job which is not the right job for you (and then having to try to do it) is definitely worse, and it is not good for the school either.

Questions for reflection

Consider the type of school you want to lead, and the reasons why you feel this kind of school is suited to your temperament, skill set, experience, educational vision and values. It could be:

- A primary school, secondary school, an all-age school or post-16 setting.

- A mainstream school, special school or alternative provision.

- A secular school or faith school.

- A state school or an independent school.

- A UK school or an international school.

- A day school, boarding school or day/boarding combination.

- A single-sex or co-educational school.

- A comprehensive or selective school.

- A school within a local authority, an academy, free school or specialist school (such as a university technical college).

- Of a particular size.

- Of a particular social or ethnic mix.

■ Serving a particular type of community (e.g. leafy suburb or inner city).

■ Within a specific geographical area, or you may be mobile/flexible.

In each case, justify your thinking. Why will this school type suit you? In what way would you suit this particular type of school?

Finally, is this an internal position or an external position? Internally promoted headships offer a particular range of challenges and a number of opportunities. I shall address both in the forthcoming chapters, but consider this at the outset: if you are a deputy who has never expressed any interest in moving on to headship, who has never undertaken any specific professional development to prepare for making the move and who has never applied for headships of other schools, are you a credible candidate if the headship of your current school falls vacant and you decide to apply? Can you convince the governing body that you are the strongest contender for the role, and that your reluctance to apply for other headships stems from the fact that this is the only school you would want to lead? Can you demonstrate that, although being established within the school (and the longer you have been in post the more difficult this may be), you can still see the school with fresh eyes and, in particular, its capacity for growth and development? You may need to counter the more objective perspective of external applicants who will, in addition, bring with them experiences and insights from other schools which might strengthen their applications. Can you convincingly persuade the selection panel that the school will do better under your leadership than anyone else's? If you believe you can, and you definitely want the job, go for it.

Having considered the questions for reflection above, you should have a clearer sense of the kind of school you would wish to lead, and why. It should enable you to go on to identify vacancies which fulfil your criteria. You are then in a position to begin your research into specific schools and to prepare yourself to make a strong application. Although an element of this process has been about choosing a leadership context which appeals to you, your chief task during the selection and appointment process is to convince the recruitment panel of what you have to contribute, rather than what you have to gain. My advice would be to think (and talk) in terms of what you would bring to the role and the school.

So how do you do that? You have two opportunities to convince the selection panel that you are the best fit for the role/school: first through your written application, and second through your performance at interview. Your written references should then serve to reinforce your application, confirming that your prior experience and achievements marry with the claims you have made about your aptitude and potential as a school leader.

Making a strong written application

Completing a job application is a time-consuming process, but my strong advice would be to make sure you devote sufficient care and thought to it. Tempting though it may be to have a generic letter of application which you tweak to fit a new vacancy, such letters rarely impress. It is often very clear when candidates have simply used the 'find and replace' option to change the school name. Indeed, as a head I have seen applications where occasionally the name of the previous school a candidate applied to has not been changed. Needless to say, I did not meet such candidates at interview.

If you are a senior leader you will already have successfully applied for promoted posts in the past. It may be that much of the advice I offer in this chapter is something you have already considered, and indeed implemented, earlier in your career. I may make suggestions with which you disagree or which you do not believe will work in your context, but this is all useful food for reflection as you negotiate the application process. Do consider, however, that headship is a significant step up, and preparing an application for an audience of governors is different in a number of ways from targeting your application at a head teacher, a fellow educational professional, which is what you will no doubt have done prior to this point. Although I think the issue of match/fit to the school and the role will have featured in earlier decisions about which positions you sought in the past, nowhere is this more critical than when you are readying yourself to step into the shoes of the school leader.

If, as part of the process of deciding what post/school to apply for, you have done your research into this specific school and role, then this is your starting point for making a strong written application. Your application needs to demonstrate clearly that you have thought about the needs of this particular school at this point in its educational journey. You have given time and thought to what this school might need from its next head (how can it build on its past successes and achieve even more in the future?), and you have afforded careful consideration to how you are the best person to lead it from this point onwards so that it capitalises on opportunities and faces inevitable challenges from a position of strength. No school stands still; if it tries to do so, it slips backwards. Reflecting on my own teaching and leadership career since 1980 I can confidently say that the one constant over that time has been change.

So start from where the school is, rather than starting from where you are. Think about what the school needs from its incoming leader, and go on to demonstrate in a clear and compelling way that you fit the bill. In fact, you are a better fit than any other contender – including internal applicants if you are an external candidate, and vice versa. Not only do you have to be a credible candidate who is worth inviting to interview, but you also need to go into the process with the conviction that you are the best candidate they will see.

Of course, this requires a significant degree of confidence on your part! To be clear, you are not claiming to be perfect, to have all the answers or to be the finished article. You recognise, as I explored in the introduction (remember Robert Quinn's phrase about 'building the bridge as you walk on it'), that to an extent you learn how to do a job by doing a job. However, you can convince the panel that you are adaptable, conscientious, receptive to learning from experience and committed to building your skills and increasing your capability over time. You have the fundamental temperament, approach and outlook that will enable you to do this well. You want to be challenged and to grow as a result. Every job you have ever taken on will no doubt have required you to tackle areas of responsibility and demanding tasks which have been new to you. But you have done so successfully and you are proud of what you have achieved as a result. You show through this that you have the transferable skills, the character and the determination to make a success of headship – specifically this headship in this school at this time.

It is also worth considering that there will be a period of time between being appointed and taking up the role, and this 'lead-in' period, as I have called it, offers opportunities to reinforce your skills further. It may be that there are elements of the 'desirable' section of the person specification (or even the 'essential' section) which you are still working on, but, if successful, this is something you could prioritise during the lead-in period. It might be worth exploring this in your letter. Further information about how to make the best use of the lead-in period follows in Chapter 3.

One of the most compelling letters of application I ever received was from a candidate for the position of business manager in the school where I was the head. This candidate actually constructed his application according to his 'RAG' rating. He coloured green the elements of the role for which he was applying that he felt he was already strong in (and clearly explained why); he coloured amber those areas where he felt he was still building his skills (and explained how he would further strengthen them in the time between appointment and officially assuming the role). He only had one area he had identified as 'red'. This was health and safety, something which had never formed part of his professional responsibilities in the past. However, he had already identified an appropriate certificated course which he committed to completing during the lead-in period, should he be successful in his application. He was successful, he completed the health and safety course before he started and he went on to be an exceptional school business manager.

Be aware that if, when you come to draft the application, you find it incredibly difficult, if not impossible, to demonstrate that you are a good match for what the post requires, this tells you something. Or if, as you try to put your case, you find your own enthusiasm and conviction ebbing rather than building, that may be revealing, too. It is important that we have self-belief, confidence without arrogance and self-assurance which is not complacency. Yes, we should be aware that headship is a significant step up from being a deputy, and it will tax and test us. But we should feel more excited than daunted. If this is not the case, perhaps this is not the right time. Trust the judgement of mentors and role models who know you well and whose opinion you respect. If the head in the school where you are a deputy has been supportive and positively invested in preparing you for this step, then make the most of their professional insight. Have faith in their faith in you, and let that encourage you to believe in your capacity to make the leap. If the head you currently work with has not been supportive and does not show this confidence in you – and/or you are a valuable deputy they do not wish to lose – you will clearly need to be more self-sufficient and personally motivated. Perhaps you need to get a headship and do it well (better than they have done?) to prove how capable you are, both to them and to yourself.

Too many letters of application, in my experience, read simply as 'a list of what I have done in the past'. If you think about it, what has happened in your professional past is of far less significance than what could happen in your professional future. In your letter of application you need to be able to convince the selectors of your potential – not of what you have done, but of what you could do, given the opportunity. Your past experiences and achievements are simply the examples which will illustrate and strengthen your claims about your transferable skills.

Start from the details you have about the job and the school. Take advantage of the opportunity to visit the school and gather information from that – but just be aware that from the moment you set foot in the building (and, in fact, from your initial contact with the school, for example, by email or in a telephone conversation) you will be judged, weighed and measured. In effect, the selection process starts here. Show that you are listening and learning. Show your interest in, and your respect for, what the school is achieving and has achieved, including the contribution of the outgoing head. Ensure you develop a clear sense of its strengths, as well as beginning to hone your perceptions of what it might do even better in the future. Make sure that, through your research and your visit, you develop a very clear sense of the ethos and climate of the school, its principles, priorities and current systems, and how it lives its vision and values in its day-to-day processes and relationships.

One of the concepts I was introduced to through my doctoral reading was the concept of appreciative enquiry, an improvement model which begins by focussing on what is going well and considers what can be learnt from this which could raise the bar elsewhere. This links with Chip and Dan Heath's emphasis on 'finding the bright spots' in *Switch: How to Change Things When Change Is Hard* (2010). According to Chip and Dan Heath, when hoping to make improvements we focus too much on finding what is broken and trying to fix it, rather than identifying what is going well and doing more of it. A headship candidate needs to find the right balance between recognising a school's strengths and ensuring those are acknowledged and further developed, while at the same time showing awareness of the potential for growth and the areas in which provision can be enhanced. Certainly, a selection panel of governors who are loyal to the school and emotionally invested in its performance will not welcome an application which appears to be full of criticism of the current regime. In addition, building your relationship with the current head who, if all goes well, you will succeed, begins here, and it is in everyone's interests, including the interests of the school itself, if the dynamic between incoming and outgoing heads is as positive as possible.

So, assuming you have identified a school whose leadership you aspire to, consider the following:

- Visit the school and learn from the process.

- Do systematic research to find out as much as you can about the school and the role, including going through the information pack, the job description and person specification with a fine-toothed comb, checking the website, prospectus, reading all the information you can find online and offline – for example, the last school magazine, if they produce one, and scrutinising its most recent inspection report.

- If this is an independent school within the Independent Schools Council, and also a charity, check its entry on the Charity Commission website: https://www.gov.uk/government/organisations/ charity-commission.

- Make notes on the school's current strengths and its areas for development.

- Reflect on what you think the school needs from its next head teacher.

You are then in a position to begin to draft your application.

Look carefully at what the application process requires. Usually the completion of a specific form is mandatory, with the option to include a more detailed supporting statement/letter. Sometimes a CV will also be required, but in other cases this is seen as simply duplicating information within the form and it is made explicit that CVs are not to be included. Look at all the documents you are enclosing in your application pack as a whole and avoid repetition/duplication where you can. Stick to word limits if they are specified. Ensure the information you include is succinctly expressed, clear, fluent and accurate; it is a good idea to ask others to read, reflect and give you feedback. You must ensure that everything you send is thoroughly proofread and contains no typographical errors or inaccuracies in grammar, punctuation or spelling.

It may be that you are asked to enclose additional papers addressing given subjects, and this is likely to require some research and considerable thought. The issues they ask you to address will, of course, give you further information about the school's priorities and, perhaps, current concerns, so this should be useful to you as you prepare for possible discussion of key issues at interview.

Before adding referees' details to the application form, ensure that you have, as a courtesy, checked that they are happy to provide a reference for you. If there is any reason why your first referee is not your current employer, you need to have a narrative to explain this. Occasionally applicants request that referees are not contacted unless the candidate is shortlisted, which suggests that they have not yet discussed their application with their current employer. Although I do understand the reason for this, it always makes me a little uneasy. You may wish your employer/referee to keep the process confidential within your school, and that is acceptable. However, applying for a job without the foreknowledge of your current employer is a different proposition. I would suggest that it is always better to be transparent with job applications rather than secretive. I accept that this may depend on the relationship you have with your current head and their attitude towards, and support of, your career ambitions.

In terms of demonstrating future potential and showing a clear match between the job details and your application, my advice is to start with the different areas of responsibility and the skills and aptitudes specified by the selection panel. Is it possible to structure your supporting letter so that you deal directly with these elements of the job for which you are applying? Actually using, in places, phrases from the job description/person specification shows that you are targeting this particular role in this particular school, rather than simply adapting and regurgitating an application you have prepared in connection with a completely different role. Think in terms of:

The post requires the successful applicant to assume responsibility for X.

This requires skill Y.

I have skill Y, or the capacity to develop it, as shown by my achievements in Z.

In this way, the application presents a compelling argument for your suitability for this post, rather than simply detailing what you have done in the past. It ensures that you select from the different experiences and accomplishments in your career to date whatever is most relevant to this specific post. It keeps the application focussed and concise.

Be aware that this sometimes means there are achievements from earlier roles which you are proud of which you do not then include. This can be difficult, and it takes some self-discipline to leave them out. Similarly, listing every continuing professional development (CPD) opportunity you have taken in the past ten years is unlikely to be pertinent. It is far better to state 'Relevant professional development includes ...' and to go on to detail what CPD activity is most appropriate with respect to strengthening your claim that you are ready and well suited to step up to this challenge. Just be aware that some of your professional development should relate to your preparation for stepping up to a new level of responsibility. If your CPD record is dominated by activity which relates to doing your current job well, laudable though that may be, this does not reflect a commitment to moving forward professionally and being as well prepared for such a move as you possibly can be.

In addition to focussing on tasks and the requisite skills, your application also needs to give a sense of who you are and what you believe. Again, your educational philosophy and principles, your vision and values, and your sense of moral purpose need to be aligned to those of the school which you hope to join. If you find yourself saying anything which you do not believe in order to show you are a match to the school to which you are applying, then ask yourself whether this is the right position for you. Heads need to be adaptable and flexible. However, where principles are concerned they need to show integrity and be true to themselves. You will have to negotiate a new professional identity when you move into headship; it is a different role from being a deputy. But this identity has to be coherent with who you are and what you stand for. Your application should give a clear sense of this. Headship is not simply what you do. To an extent it says something important about who you are.

Remember this is a leadership position, and, of all the things you discuss in your application, you must ensure you give a strong sense of what kind of leader you are. For example, how do you strike the right balance of support and challenge in your relationships with those you lead? How do you earn and build trust? How do you win hearts and minds? How can you encourage and inspire others to be their best? Have you shown moral courage in your previous leadership roles? Have you shown sensitivity to, and adaptability to, context? Consider how you have achieved success as a leader in the past (cite specific examples which your references should confirm), and how headship will allow you (and require you) to do this in a different way. Are you fully aware of what makes headship different from being a deputy, both in terms of its challenges and its opportunities? How will you address the former and make the most of the latter?

When you have drafted your application go back through your research and cross-check. Have you covered all the key elements of the job details? Have you effectively demonstrated that there is a match between your temperament, skills, experience, achievements and potential and what the selectors are clearly looking for? Have you given a clear sense of your vision and values? If *you* were on the selection panel, would you be inviting this particular applicant for interview? Would you be sufficiently interested in what they have to say to want to meet them to find out more?

I would suggest that if you are an internal candidate, all of the above still applies. Do not fall into the trap of failing to mention achievements, successes or key strengths because you believe 'they will know this'. Make it very clear that you are a good match for the role, with your conviction that this is the case reinforced by your existing knowledge of the school. Show that you have ideas and initiative, and that appointing you will not mean simply maintaining a status quo. No school can afford to stand still.

Questions for reflection

- Have you demonstrated your understanding of the needs of this specific school at this particular point in its history?

- Have you achieved a balance between recognising the school's strengths and achievements while also identifying possible areas for further development and growth?

- Have you made a very clear connection between what will be required from the next head of the school and what you have to offer, as evidenced by examples of what you have experienced and accomplished in the past?

- Have you shown that, where the job requires you to take on areas of responsibility which are new to you, you have transferable skills or the capacity to build the relevant skills? Have you shown your commitment to continuing to learn?

- Does your educational philosophy come through clearly in your application, and is it aligned with what, according to your research, the school believes in and prioritises?

- While addressing all the elements of the position applied for, and your own core values, have you still been able to keep your application concise and succinctly expressed?

- Are you confident that it is clearly expressed, jargon-free, and fluently and accurately written, having checked this, if necessary, with a skilful proofreader? Have you taken care not to overuse acronyms, particularly as this application will be going to some governors who may not be as well versed in edu-speak as you are? Educators often use acronyms such as CPD, SEN and PSHE without even thinking about it. (G&T may mean something quite different to some of your readers.)

■ Have you asked for honest, objective feedback from professionals whose judgement you respect, preferably with them commenting on your application alongside the job details and person specification?

When you have reflected on all these points, you may be ready to send off the application and, if successfully short-listed, to begin to prepare yourself for the interview stage of the selection process.

Preparing for and performing well at interview

All the work you have done so far – researching the role and school before planning, writing and checking your application – will serve you well as you move into the next stage – preparing for, and subsequently performing well at, interview. If you are thoroughly prepared, well informed about this position and this context, and secure in your perception that you are a strong, credible candidate who is capable of making a success of this role, then that should give you confidence as you move into the interview stage of the selection process.

However, interviews are nerve-wracking situations (and in some respects quite unnatural – when would you normally focus on convincing those around you of how good you are?), and a degree of anxiety is perhaps inevitable. It is also, to some extent, healthy. Remember that the key is to show self-belief, confidence without arrogance and self-assurance which is not complacency. I am firmly of the belief that a degree of humility and self-doubt makes us stronger leaders rather than weaker ones: the leaders who cause me concern are the ones who never seem to show any self-doubt at all. So, at stages of the process you may feel nervous, and you may even at times question your own worth. If you are fully prepared you can minimise any potentially damaging effect of this and ensure that you are still able to give a convincing, compelling account of your suitability for the post.

A degree of fatalism is no bad thing. Interviewing is certainly not an exact science, and selection panels sometimes get it wrong. However, sometimes you are not the best candidate for a particular role, even though you may not see it. I have been a disappointed interview candidate fourteen times in my teaching career – and there were, of course, countless times when I applied for posts and did not even reach the interview stage. Looking back, some of the jobs I failed to get were perhaps not the right jobs at the right time for me, although I felt they were when I applied. As a headship candidate, in particular, it is crucial that you know the appointment panel has faith in your capacity to do the job and to do it well. You wouldn't want to work for a governing body that didn't choose you.

You have to be able to cope with disappointment and not to let it derail you. If headship is a role you are keen to do, the right job will be out there, and it is, of course, crucial that you keep looking. If you start to doubt your capacity to do the job following a string of rejections, go back to your mentors and role models – people who know you well and have a clear sense of your current capacity and future potential, and ideally people who also have some understanding of the demands and opportunities of headship. If they believe in your ability to step up to headship, take reassurance from that. They will know you better than a selection panel who met you over one or two days. But that selection panel will have met a range of candidates, and it may well be that one of them was a better match for what that school needs now. Perhaps the skills they brought to the role complemented the existing skills of the senior staff and governors more successfully than your own skills did. Do what you need to do to come to terms with disappointment, and get back on the horse. It is certainly the case that if you are not prepared to risk failure, and not resilient enough to cope with it, you will not achieve success.

Remember, too, that when you are appointing staff, for every successful candidate who is delighted to be chosen, there are several who are rejected. You need to be able to understand that perspective and to appreciate their pain. In one of my senior jobs, the head was retiring and I was asked to meet the shortlisted headship candidates over lunch. One of them told me he had never been interviewed for a job he had not been offered. Perhaps I only inferred a degree of smugness and arrogance in this comment, but I found myself hoping that this might be his first experience of failure. It seemed to me that heads, in particular, should bear the scars of earlier disappointment to strengthen their sense of empathy with those who do not succeed in the appointment process. (This candidate was not appointed to the headship.)

So what can you do to improve your chances of success and to ensure you are fully prepared for and able to perform as well as you can at interview?

Look back at the information you collected at the stage of deciding whether to apply, which you used (clearly to good effect) in your written application. Ideally you should already have visited the school, which will have given you the opportunity to meet people and to begin to develop your knowledge and understanding of its priorities, ethos and culture – 'the way things are done here' and why. This will be the raw material you will work with if you are appointed, the legacy you step into and which you will build on. It should have confirmed that this school and this role are a good fit for you, and vice versa. Remember, it is all about 'match'. Your task through the selection process is to demonstrate, convincingly, that you are the right person to fulfil this role in such a way as to enable the school to thrive in the future. Depending on the context, this may require significant dramatic change, gentle evolution or, in most cases, something in-between.

In all your previous interviews within the world of education, the chances are the main person you have been trying to convince of your suitability for the post is the head teacher. You have been talking to a fellow educator, someone who may well have already fulfilled the kind of position for which you are applying, and who, certainly in the vast majority of cases, began their career, as you probably did, as a classroom teacher. Your main audience now may be a group of governors – volunteers with a range of types of expertise and from different backgrounds, committed to the school but perhaps without the depth of understanding of education that you have taken for granted in the past. As I observed in the section on making a strong written application, you need to watch the language you use, such as an unthinking reliance on acronym shorthand. The governors will expect you to have expertise in education, but blinding them with science at interview is not a good strategy.

So an understanding and appreciation of the perspective of your audience is important. There may well be members of your governing body who do have a background in education (although it might be in a context other than schools), and there may also be members of the panel, additional to the governing body, who have specialist educational knowledge. Depending on the school type, this could be representatives from a local authority, from an overarching trust or foundation, from a professional search firm or perhaps an independent educational adviser. Most governing bodies are accustomed to delegating much important work to the head and their senior staff. Suddenly they are faced with, arguably, their most significant challenge – appointing the next head of the school. They cannot delegate this to the outgoing school leader. They may well look elsewhere for expertise they can draw on and educational advice they can source.

The process they go through will also depend on a range of factors, including the advice they have received and the school's context. The norm is probably to bring in a larger group of candidates at the long-list stage, which is then reduced to a smaller field for the final shortlist interviews. There may well be a number of 'in-tray' exercises to complete at some point, and these are tasks it is difficult to prepare for as they require you to demonstrate that you are quick-thinking and can exercise good judgement within pressured time constraints, mirroring, albeit in an artificial and contrived way, some of the challenges of school leadership.

In addition to the formal panel interview and making a presentation, you may be asked to do some of the following:

- Take part in a number of small panel interviews – for example, with a specific focus on leadership and management or teaching and learning.

- Lead an assembly.

- Teach (which could be in your own school).

- Address the whole staff, or a section of them, with a general brief or a specific focus.

- Chair a meeting of staff who are in role rather than being themselves.

- Address the selection panel as though they were staff and introduce your first staff meeting.

- Address the staff as if they were parents or prospective parents.

- Talk to student representatives, which might take the form of a question and answer session with the school council or with senior students.

- Draft a written response to an issue, such as a parental complaint (which could be handwritten and so without a grammar or spellcheck facility).

- Write a general letter of introduction to the parent community.

- Draft email replies to a range of contentious issues, making clear which should take priority, where you would delegate and where you would act.

- Observe a lesson and feed back to the teacher.

- Conduct a learning walk and then report to the panel on what you learnt – your initial impressions and possible areas for development.

- Carry out a data exercise or financial task – for example, identifying budget priorities, which might be followed by drafting a brief written report for the governors.

The range of potential tasks and activities is wide. In every case, consider the key skills they are looking for and what it is they may be trying to find out about your temperament, your principles and your leadership style. It may be that the tasks you undergo are not significantly different from the challenges you have faced in your senior leader role. As far as possible, it is important to do what you *would* do were you in that situation. In my view, it is a mistake to try to second-guess the panel and to say or do what you believe they are looking for. If this is not the right job/context for you, that should emerge during the interview process. Remember, not getting a job is not the worst thing that can happen; getting the wrong job might be.

If you are an internal candidate and you are offered any choices about how far you follow the same programme as any external candidates, including, for example, having a tour of the school, my advice would be to go through the same process your fellow candidates are experiencing, however artificial this might seem. It is useful to be exposed to exactly what your fellow interviewees are going through. Bear in mind that, if you are not successful in the process, you may be working very closely with one of them. It is in everyone's interests for positive relationships to be built from the outset.

Whatever additional tasks or exercises you are presented with, the two elements which are usually part of the process are the formal panel interview and making a presentation. Consider how you might prepare for each of these and what you need to remember during that stage of the selection process.

With respect to the formal panel interview, my advice is to go through all the information you have about the school and the role again, thoroughly. Ask yourself what you might want to ask if you were a member of the selection panel. What questions might enable you to probe whether the candidates before you were strong contenders for this position? What questions would elicit whether the 'essentials' and 'desirables' of the person specification were duly satisfied? Compile a full list of potential questions based on the job description and accompanying details.

Now go through your own application, together with any additional statements or papers. Although an appointment panel should use the same structured questions with each candidate, there may be follow-up questions which relate to some of the things you have said in writing. Consider whether you can think of specific questions which connect to what you have included in your written application. What might you be asked to expand on? Are there any claims you might be called upon to justify? Add these to your growing list of potential questions.

Finally, consider what you picked up on during your visit and through all the reading and research you have done thus far. What do you think they are really interested in? What would you be expecting, or wanting, the incoming head to focus on if you were already a member of this school community? What questions would enable you to identify whether the candidate in front of you was sufficiently astute and alert to have spotted these things, and whether they have specific ideas which could support the school as it moves forward? Add these questions to your list.

If you have done all this thoroughly, you should now have a substantial list of possible questions. So what might your responses be? How will you ensure your answers to such questions are considered and compelling? What examples might you draw on from your own experience to strengthen your answers? Draft out possible replies to the different questions. Ensure they are relevant, well expressed and succinct. Answer the question and then stop – so obvious, but not always easy! Don't repeat yourself and don't drift off the point. If you find some questions more taxing than others, leave them for now and come back to them later. Continue with the exercise until you consider you have thought through and planned out good answers to all the questions you anticipated.

Then practise. It is possible to practise on your own, just getting used to verbalising your answers and hearing how they sound. Perhaps record your answers, then play them back and listen carefully to how you come across. Leave it a while and then try it again. Eventually you should be able to do this without any notes or prompts, and your confidence should build with the experience of the practice.

If you have someone to work with you on this, firing questions, including follow-up questions that you may not have anticipated and giving you feedback on your responses afterwards, this is even more useful. It may be a friend or family member who is not an educationalist; remember your answers have to be intelligible and convincing to someone who isn't as steeped in the world of education as you are. Again, it is good to try the exercise more than once with some time in-between. You should find that your facility in answering the questions improves.

You should have considered answers to a far greater number and wider range of questions than you will actually be presented with in the formal panel interview itself, but in my view this is all time well spent. It encourages reflection and careful consideration. It helps you to think through what is relevant and most significant. The practice gives you the opportunity to try out responses and to hear how they sound. Think about the pace at which you are speaking, how well modulated your voice is, how fluent you are – can you avoid the 'fillers' and hesitations of 'erm' and mannerisms such as 'like' and 'sort of'? We often use such words without even realising it – recording yourself and listening to it afterwards, or seeking feedback from someone else, can help you to judge more objectively how fluently you are speaking. You will, of course, be tested on both the quality of your ideas and the quality of your delivery. You need to work on both at the planning stage.

Just as when we prepare students for examinations, we have to help them to see that of all the things they know about a topic, and ideally all the things they have revised, only a proportion will ultimately be required – but they don't know which proportion, so the fuller their preparation is, the safer they will be. In the examination they have to be selective, applying what they have learnt to the question under consideration. So it will be for you. In the panel interview, although you may inevitably be nervous, you need to listen extremely carefully and ensure you answer the specific question posed, and not a (perhaps similar) question you had anticipated and prepared for. And although I fully believe this thorough preparation is the right thing to do, of course, in the interview you need to sound natural and not over-rehearsed. You have to establish the most positive relationship with the panel and show warmth, humanity and the capacity to make a connection in addition to passion, commitment and conviction. This can actually be an enjoyable challenge!

Ensuring your answers are reasonably concise and you round them off properly and pause, smile, sit back and wait for the next question can be taxing. It is tempting, especially when you are anxious, to talk too quickly, to talk at too great a length and to repeat yourself. If you are trying to be persuasive, sometimes you can overstate your case, add too much detail and start 'telling a story'. You refer to an example of something you have experienced or achieved to illustrate a claim you have made or an idea you have expressed, and several minutes later you find you are still recounting what happened or what you did. Answer the question. Then stop. If the panel want you to expand on your answer, they will ask you to do so.

It is not unusual for the panel members themselves to experience a degree of anxiety. They have a number of candidates to see, a number of questions to get through, a process to follow. If you are unable to answer concisely, you can increase their anxiety. They need to stick to their schedule. When you practise, ensure you rehearse rounding off answers so that you are not tempted to ramble.

You are likely to be asked at the end of the formal interview whether you have any further questions. Make sure you have given this some thought. It is quite acceptable to say that you have had a positive, informative day, and all the questions you arrived with have been answered as the day has gone on. But it is also a good idea to have a couple of specific, thoughtful questions that you have kept in reserve for this point – questions that show you are astute, that you have picked up a significant amount during your time at the school and that you would use this building knowledge to make an impact if you were appointed. However, I would counsel against any questions which might make the selection panel defensive. And certainly don't say, 'I prepared a number earlier,' and draw out a long list. The panel were starting to gear themselves up for the next candidate.

So, if you prepare thoroughly, practise conscientiously and give yourself thinking time so that your answers are carefully considered, fluently expressed and succinct, you should have the opportunity to impress the panel as someone who is committed, thoughtful and confident. Try not to worry too much if you feel nervous – it is natural – but if necessary think about your breathing and take even breaths (not necessarily deep breaths but regular, even breaths – count if it helps), which can have a calming effect. Listen carefully, and don't be afraid to ask for a question to be repeated if you need it. Be prepared to give yourself a slight pause to gather your thoughts, too. This is better than an inadequately considered answer.

If you have to make a formal presentation to the panel or to a wider audience, this may be on a subject which you are given in advance with plenty of time to research and prepare – for example, you may be told this when you are notified that you have progressed to the final shortlist stage. Alternatively, you may be given the subject very shortly before the presentation itself, with only a short block of time (for example, half an hour) to ready yourself mentally. These two different situations clearly test slightly different things. In the latter case it is likely that the presentation will be less polished but, of course, more spontaneous. Sometimes you will be able to use technology/visual aids and sometimes you may be asked not to do so. They may want you to keep it simple – they are looking at and listening to you.

In some cases candidates may be asked what they would like to talk about, so they have a free choice of subject. This would give you the opportunity to select a topic which is of relevance to the school at this stage of its journey, drawing on all the research and preparation you have done and showing that you are tuning in to this specific context. You will also obviously wish to choose a subject about which you can show enthusiasm and in an area where you have particular interest and expertise.

With respect to topics which might be given to you, consider the following subjects which I have known headship candidates be asked to present on:

- Challenges and opportunities for the school over the next five years.

- Moving from good to outstanding (not simply in terms of inspection judgements but in the sense of ensuring the school is the best it can be in all areas).

- How your vision would underpin the school ethos and help the school improve.

- Closing the gap between the achievements of different groups of pupils.

- Ensuring pupils make the most successful transitions from one stage of their education to another (e.g. primary to secondary, Key Stage 3 to Key Stage 4, at 16-plus and beyond 18).

- How you envisage your first 100 days in post.

- What your key priorities would be as incoming head.

If you are given a precise time limit, then prepare carefully and practise thoroughly so that you can keep the presentation within that time frame. Do not assume that they will be flexible here: sometimes a selection panel will give you a one-minute warning and then stop the presentation when the specified time has elapsed, which can throw you if you overrun. My advice would be to prepare the presentation as fully as you can, with whatever planning time you are given. Convert your initial full notes into much briefer ones and use those as a guide in the presentation itself; it is important that you speak to your audience rather than read at them – make eye contact, smile, continue to build a connection with them.

The panel will, of course, be interested in the content of what you say, and that should be thoughtful and appropriate to the school's context. Show how much you have learnt from the time of first seeing the advertisement for the post and use this knowledge to good effect now. If you are asked to talk about what specific changes you would make (and this may happen in the formal panel interview too), just be circumspect; it might sound arrogant to be too definitive about what you feel needs to change, and how that might happen, on the basis of your acquaintance with the school so far. Until you are actually in post, listening and learning and working closely alongside governors and staff, you will not be in a position to make sweeping statements about large-scale change. Similarly, if you are asked about vision and values, your own vision and values are important and should be clear and communicated in a compelling way. But remember that no incoming head imposes their vision and values on the school they move to lead. They inherit a school ethos and culture which will, under their leadership, evolve over time. Be aware of this and talk about your general educational philosophy, sense of moral purpose and core beliefs, and relate those to the school as you see it.

It is important to talk positively about the school as it is now – remember, these are governors who are likely to be emotionally invested in the school – while still being aware of opportunities to develop and improve. Remember Chip and Dan Heath's 'bright spots' and recognising, valuing and using successes – every school will have them, whatever challenges it faces – rather than seeing yourself as the leader who will sweep away all that has gone before and start from scratch. I would suggest that even in a school which requires dramatic transformation, there will be good staff and some effective practice which should be appreciated and not overlooked.

In addition to the content of the presentation, the panel will be evaluating your style. Do you come across well to the audience, and can they envisage you successfully addressing groups of pupils, staff, parents, prospective parents and members of the wider community? Can you instil a sense of confidence in your audience, whoever they might be and whatever the subject and context of a presentation? Although you may be nervous, are you able to speak in such a way that you make a connection and build positive relationships? Are you interesting and compelling to listen to?

Following the presentation, it is usual to face questions from the panel. Consider this when planning and rehearsing – anticipate what they could ask and how you could respond. If you practise in front of someone else, ask them to think of and ask questions at the end, in addition to giving you feedback. How clear and fluent were you? Did you speak at an appropriate pace, and was your voice well modulated so that it was not monotonous, leading to your audience's attention possibly drifting? Was it well structured and logical? Did you stick to the time limit? If appropriate, was there warmth and humour in it? Did you make eye contact with the audience, use positive body language and effectively make a connection with your listeners? Can your audience of one suggest further ways in which the presentation could be improved?

Finally, whatever the outcome of the selection process, ensure you have learnt from it. If you are successful, consider how much better prepared you are now to take up the reins of this particular headship than you were before you first saw the advertisement. If you are disappointed, reflect on whether, in fact, this was the right post in the right school at the right time. If you are convinced it was, find a way to come to terms with your disappointment. (Would you want to work alongside a governing body that weren't astute enough to recognise your potential? If they didn't choose you, they don't deserve you!) Do not allow it to derail you and deter you from future applications, no matter how bruised you might feel and how badly your pride may have been dented. If colleagues know you are going through the process, it can be difficult to go back into your school (sometimes on a significant number of occasions) having been unsuccessful. Being a frustrated internal candidate can be especially painful (someone, somewhere, was running a book on whether you would get it ...). But if you have the capacity to be a head, the temperament, the developing skills, the positive attitude and approach to continuing to learn and grow, then the right job is out there. Show your strength; build your resilience; do not give up.

I would always recommend that, if you are unsuccessful, you ask for feedback. Some schools are cagey about supplying it, perhaps fearing that they may be challenged or may make themselves in some way vulnerable if they seek to justify their decisions. Some schools may give you nothing, or very little, or bland statements which take you no further. However, you may receive meaningful, specific and detailed feedback which helps you to learn even more from the experience and which you can use to strengthen future applications.

Questions for reflection

If you are at this stage of your leadership journey, reflect on the following:

- Is the job you are considering applying for a good match for what you have to bring to the role/ school?

- Are you prepared to spend the time and effort required to do your research and to plan your written application thoroughly, rather than simply tweaking a previous application and hoping for the best?

- Can you ensure you approach the interview process with the same diligence and conscientious strategy? Whatever the outcome, you need to feel confident that you did your best, and, if you were not successful on this occasion, it was because of factors beyond your control rather than because you did not do justice to your potential.

- If you are successful, can you recognise that all you have learnt during the process will serve you well both in the lead-in period prior to officially taking up the post and in your early weeks and months?

■ If you are unsuccessful, have you spent time reflecting on what you have learnt and how this might enable you to submit a stronger application for the next vacancy to which you consider you are suited? If feedback was offered, have you made the most of it?

In the next chapter I shall consider the lead-in period between being successful in the selection process and officially taking up the role – the time between 'getting the badge' and 'sitting in the chair'. From tracking the progress of my six research participants and analysing the nature of the transition through which they were passing, I recognised that this is a crucial time. Used well, it can make a significant difference to your chances of making a positive beginning in the role.

Managing the lead-in period

The challenges of finding the balance in the period between appointment and formally taking up the role

The most difficult promotion I managed to secure in my career was moving from second in English to head of English, a transition I eventually made in 1989. I had my first interview for the role of head of department in 1987, however, and over the next two years I was interviewed nine times. The final interview resulted in successful appointment.

I was 29 and newly married. We had been given two good bottles of champagne as one of our wedding presents and had decided we would save them for future special occasions. I was unaware that each time I left for an interview, my husband would put one of the bottles to chill in the fridge. Each time I came home, dejected and on several occasions in tears, he had to sneak the bottle out of the fridge, back up the stairs and under the bed in the spare room before I saw it. When we finally opened the bottle in celebration in 1989, he told me what had happened. I seem to remember him saying something about his fears that it might end up being 'vintage'.

79

In retrospect, not all the jobs I was interviewed for during that two-year period were necessarily the right jobs in the right school at the right time – but I felt they were. And once you are 'in the zone' and start applying and being interviewed, you want to be successful. This can blind you to the fact that, perhaps, this isn't the best time or the most fitting post.

I think I was fortunate in that the head of English role I secured in 1989 was a good match for me – one in which I was happy and, I believe, successful. But I think that was possibly good luck rather than good management.

I remember at that time reading a poem by Roger McGough called 'The Leader' where the narrator's excitement about becoming a leader is deflated in the final line: 'OK. What shall we do?' I also remember a cartoon I had seen which I copied and posted up in the staffroom to tell my colleagues that I had (finally) secured a head of department post. In the first four frames, a woman celebrates getting a job – with her workmates, friends and family, with champagne, balloons and streamers. In the final frame she sits alone with her head in her hands and the caption is: 'Now I have to DO the job …'

Despite having finally secured a job I had been pursuing for two years, my feelings were fluctuating constantly. I certainly experienced excitement and exhilaration at having landed a job I really wanted, felt excited by and ready for. However, this alternated with feelings of apprehension and trepidation about the nature of the task ahead. Two members of my new department had also been interviewed for the post, and I knew they would be dealing with their disappointment at not being successful, so establishing the most positive and productive relationship with them was likely to be an early challenge. I was the youngest member of the department and so had actually been teaching for fewer years than anyone else in the team I was to lead – although I wouldn't say this meant that I was 'the least experienced'. (When I arrived at the school I discovered that I was also actually the second youngest member on the entire teaching staff.) I expected the task ahead would tax me and stretch me, and part of me looked forward to that, while part of me felt anxious about it.

The fact that I'd had so many unsuccessful interviews for head of English over the previous two years (and on a number of other occasions I had applied and not reached the interview stage) was not helpful here. At some level this plants the idea that perhaps you are not up to the job – something the earlier selection panels astutely identified and the panel you convinced somehow missed. I even had the occasional thought that I had misheard or misunderstood when I thought they were offering me the post!

So, once you have been appointed to your headship, an early challenge may be dealing with the kind of fluctuating feelings I have described, and accepting that this may be quite a common and understandable part of the process of making a professional transition. The lead-in time between the point at which you are offered the post and the day you formally step into the role brings with it both opportunities and challenges, and this chapter will deal with both. How can you make the most of the opportunities, and how can you ensure you anticipate the challenges and prepare to meet them to the best of your ability?

The idea of finding an appropriate and workable balance is key.

- You need to achieve a balance between fulfilling your current deputy role conscientiously and giving some time and thought to the role you will soon be stepping into.

- You need a balance between being sufficiently involved in the life of your new school without being overly intrusive or insensitive to the fact that your predecessor is still the head until the end of August (if this is an autumn term start).

- You need to establish a balance between your own personal and professional responsibilities as you try to find the time to learn and prepare for the future without neglecting your own well-being or your personal relationships.

- You may also find that you are balancing fluctuating feelings of eager anticipation and acute apprehension.

The developing relationship with your predecessor

The dynamic between you and the head you succeed can be a tricky one to navigate. You need to establish as positive a rapport as you can with your predecessor, but this is a process which you cannot fully control. Much depends on the attitude and approach of the outgoing head to their own transition — either to another headship or, if they are retiring or choosing an alternative path at this stage, out of headship altogether.

It may be helpful to think about their perspective and to empathise with their position at this point in their lives. This should inform and support you as you work out how best to negotiate the relationship.

Questions for reflection

- Is your predecessor moving on to another headship, and so, like you, trying to balance their current weighty responsibilities with their increasing preoccupation with what lies ahead?

- If this is the case, are they leaving a headship where they have been generally successful, or is part of their motivation for moving on to give themselves a second (or third, or fourth) chance to make a better job of headship?

- Do the governors appear to be happy to be welcoming a new head into the school at this stage, or are they sorry and sad to see your predecessor move on? If the former, how far is the head aware of this, and how might this make them feel? If the latter, how might this manifest itself in feelings of guilt at leaving the school?

- Does the outgoing head appear to be satisfied with what they have achieved, or is there a sense that they are leaving things they have started unfinished, or moving on without having had the opportunity to tackle priorities they had earlier articulated?

■ If the head is retiring or leaving headship for an alternative career path, does this appear to be a deliberate choice on their part, or is there some reluctance to go? Have they been pressured to move on?

■ If the head has been loyal to, and emotionally invested in, the school and their role within it for the time of their tenure, how may they be coping with the change of professional identity (and status/authority) that leaving headship will represent?

■ Has the headship of the school involved a family commitment rather than just being this individual's career choice? Sometimes their children have been through the school. In boarding schools, especially, the head may have lived in a school house, so they may be leaving their family home and not simply their job. Consider the implications of this for their general state of mind at this point.

■ Do you have any sense of how the outgoing head feels about your appointment? Despite their current crucial role within the school, it is highly unlikely that they will have had significant influence over the choice of the selection panel. What might be the emotional repercussions of this? They are handing over responsibility for something they may care about greatly. Do they feel they can trust the hands into which they are placing it?

Reflecting on these questions and giving yourself the opportunity to walk around in your predecessor's shoes for a while may be a salutary experience at an early stage of your lead-in period.

There are also different views about how the lead-in period should be managed, so be wary of making assumptions that you have the same approach to it as the outgoing head. Find out what the perceptions of the governing body are, too.

In *Heads Up: The Challenges Facing England's Leading Head Teachers* (2013: 32), Dominic Carman interviews a number of high profile heads about the nature of their role. One of his interviewees talks specifically about headship as analogous to being the captain of a ship and claims: 'You'll never step on board after you've gone, and you never step on board before you start. Don't ever try. It's only your ship on the basis of your office.' Based on my own experience of assuming a headship and leaving a headship, and on my wider reading and my research with six incoming heads, I would strongly disagree with this statement. In my view, the priority here should not be the ego of the head/captain. It should be the welfare of the school/ship.

If the transition between outgoing and incoming head is not sensibly and sensitively managed, the school can suffer. The new head needs to be supported by their predecessor, governors and other senior staff to make the most positive and productive beginning to their tenure. The priority when the head changes should be how to ensure the school is energised by the change rather than damaged. Incidentally, as a former head I should also have been very disappointed if the head who succeeded me expected me never to 'step on board' after I had left. Although you may not visit the school often, it seems to me that being invited back to attend special events from time to time is appropriate and important, in recognition of the contribution you have made to the life of the school and showing that contribution is valued.

Ideally, you hope that your predecessor will be content with your appointment, and will see that helping you to build relationships with members of the school community (including the incoming intake of pupils and their families), and to learn as much as you can about the school to supplement what you already know, is in everyone's best interests and is, in fact, the last service they may perform for the school. Helping you to know, and to be known, is one way in which the head who is leaving the school can try to ensure its ongoing success.

Soon after your appointment, a visit to the school to spend some time with the outgoing head (who, in fact, you may not have met if they were not involved in the selection process) gives you the opportunity to begin to build a positive relationship with them. Together with this head and the governing body, it is useful to plan a programme of events which you might wish to incorporate into a more formal familiarisation plan. Such a plan would require you to look at the lead-in period in its entirety. When would it be appropriate for you to visit (bearing in mind that you will have significant professional commitments in your current school), and which school events would it be useful for you to attend? The outgoing head and you both need to feel comfortable with this, and to decide on how much time you will spend together on these occasions and how you will use this time.

In fact, this process can be beneficial for the head who is leaving, too, helping them to come to terms with their own transition. If they are moving on to a subsequent headship they will be balancing this with a similar process in the school to which they are moving. This can be logistically complex but, in my opinion, it needs to be properly planned, paced and systematic rather than ad hoc.

As the lead-in period goes on, the head-elect is likely to consolidate their views about what they need to know, who they would like to meet and how they would best like to use their time in the school (or perhaps out of the school but in the company of members of the school community – for example, governors, senior staff or representatives of the wider community, such as feeder schools). So it may be that as time passes you are better able to direct activity and to make specific requests of your predecessor. Certainly, several of my research participants attested to the fact that in later visits to the school they felt they were more proactive in the relationship with their predecessors and clearer about what they wished to focus on. This appears to be a natural progression as you move through the lead-in period. There may need to be a degree of assertiveness on your part as you glean from your predecessor what you feel you need to know and what you might prefer to come to your own judgement about. There is, of course, the possibility that this might not be exactly what the outgoing head wants to tell you.

It may be that the head who is leaving is seriously struggling with their move and unwilling, or even unable, to support the incoming head positively. They might be finding the imminent change in their professional identity within the school community very difficult to deal with.

There can even be a significant sense of loss/bereavement if their personal identity is very firmly bound up with their head teacher persona. Perhaps their family, too, are finding it difficult to come to terms with the dramatic change in their lives, which will inevitably increase the pressure on the outgoing head.

What if your predecessor is openly hostile (which was the situation that two of my research participants found themselves in), seeing you as almost an interloper and a threat? What if there is no sense on the part of the outgoing head that what matters is a smooth transition for the sake of the school – no appreciation that helping their successor make a positive beginning is important for the stability and ongoing confidence of the school community? What should the head-elect do?

In my experience, this is where the strength of the governors is crucial. The governing body, perhaps in conjunction with an organisation such as an overarching trust or a local authority, have appointed you. They should have confidence in you, be committed to your success and strongly invested in supporting you as you manage the transition. If the head you are succeeding is unhelpful in any way, then appealing to the chair of governors and asking for guidance and support is your best recourse.

The governors, and the trust if the school is within one, will know your predecessor far better than you do. They may well have anticipated the difficulty, which could have manifested itself at an earlier stage of the succession process. They should understand the context, the history and the full complexity of the situation. Their first loyalty should be to the school. They need to act to protect the school and to secure its future good health by ensuring that the perspective of the predecessor does not unhelpfully dominate this lead-in period. It may be that talking over the difficulties in confidence with the head of the school where you are a deputy and seeking their advice is reassuring and helpful. Be careful about discussing the situation more widely, as openly criticising your predecessor would be unprofessional, but if you are feeling frustrated and you need to talk it through, your own head teacher, assuming you have a positive relationship with them, is one potential source of support.

To make clear, I believe you should be sensitive to the position and feelings of the head you are to replace. An understanding of their point of view can be helpful, and, just as it will be in your leadership of the school, a strong sense of humanity and a dose of humility will be crucial on your part. However, you do not want the governing body to be intimidated by the outgoing head, or to be so reluctant to upset them that they fail to take responsibility and give you the support you need if you are to make effective use of the lead-in period. When your predecessor has left and you formally assume the role, you need to be in as strong a position as possible.

Two of my research participants were faced with a challenge of a different order when the heads they succeeded were eager to hand over responsibility for decisions to these incoming heads too early. These predecessors were keen to pass decisions, especially unpalatable ones, in advance of their leaving the school and the incoming head being properly established. In one case the governing body also began to make increasing demands on their newly appointed head as the lead-in period progressed. This is difficult, as you will want to impress and to show you are capable, so it is perhaps difficult to say no to the governors who appointed you or to the head you are replacing. However, you have to be careful. No matter how much you have learnt about your new school community – during your research phase, the application and interview stage, and in the months since appointment – you are still not formally in role and you must be mindful of how much there is still to learn about this specific context and the people within it. Making decisions or taking action on the basis of what you know prior to assuming the role can be a high-risk strategy. You may have to be assertive here and communicate the message that once you are in the school you will be fully committed to doing what needs to be done and to taking difficult decisions when necessary. But at this point in time the outgoing head is still the head. And if you find it difficult to say the word 'no', perhaps try 'not yet' or 'not just now'.

If you are an internally appointed new head, the situation can be particularly sensitive because, of course, you are already in situ and you know the context well. It can be the case that governors and other members of the school community start to look to you as the emerging school leader too early, with the effect that the outgoing head's position becomes increasingly untenable. The outgoing head *is* the head until the point at which they leave, and, despite your enthusiasm and eagerness to get on with the job, you have to be respectful of this throughout the lead-in time. A degree of patience is called for.

I am aware of two schools which, having appointed the new head internally, arranged sabbatical leave (which was profitably and constructively planned and used by the head-elect) so that in the final months of the outgoing head's tenure, their successor was no longer fulfilling the deputy role within the school. This can work well. However, if you are internally appointed and this sort of arrangement is not feasible, you will need to be careful not to put the head whom you have served as a deputy in an uncomfortable or unworkable position by stepping into your new role too soon, even if others are impatient to see you do so.

Whether you are externally or internally appointed, it is necessary to establish at a relatively early stage of the lead-in period exactly when the formal handover will take place. When will the outgoing head's last day in the office be? When does the incoming head officially move into it? There is no blueprint for how this should be done, but it needs to be negotiated and agreed with all concerned. In my case, I spent A level results day and the following few days in the school where I was a deputy, working with the head and staff there to support Year 13 as they made their plans for the future. The day before GCSE results I was in the school where I was taking over as head, working alongside my predecessor. She and I were also together on the morning of GCSE results – she to congratulate the Year 11 girls and to chat to their parents and the staff, while I started to get to know the year group who would be my first Year 12 cohort. At lunchtime my predecessor left the school for the last time, and I stayed.

So the relationship between the incoming and outgoing heads is important and, if it is well handled on both sides and supported by the governors, it can be instrumental to the incoming head making the most productive use of the lead-in period and the most positive beginning to their tenure as head. Once you are in post, consider how far you will involve and invite your predecessor to be part of the ongoing life of the school; this is part of their reward and, I would suggest, what they deserve in recognition of their years of service.

The opportunities of the lead-in period

If the time in-between being appointed and officially stepping into the role is used well, a significant amount of ground can be covered, which places the incoming head in a stronger position when they formally take up the post. I recommend drawing up a familiarisation plan, in conjunction with the outgoing head and your governing body, which considers the lead-in period in its entirety and how it can be used most effectively. The advantage of this short-/medium-term planning is also that you can set this against your current responsibilities and commitments in your present school, ensuring these are properly aligned so that clashes are avoided and you are not placed in the difficult position of having to choose between the two, especially at a late stage.

Ensure the head of the school where you are a deputy is consulted about this plan, and that, as far as you can influence it, they are supportive of your preparation at this stage. Two of my research participants found themselves in the situation where the head who was releasing them was grudging about their success, unhappy to have to replace them as deputies and therefore not particularly gracious about allowing these heads-elect to have time out of school. This may be something you have to accept and work round – it is difficult to challenge. In both cases my participants did manage to negotiate the situation, making full use of visits in their own time (particularly when holiday periods between their two schools fortuitously did not completely coincide so they were able to visit their new school when their current school was not in session). They made sure that when they did have leave to visit their new school they made the best possible use of their time and packed in as much productive activity as they could. It may be necessary to reassure the head where you are a deputy that you are fully committed to honouring your current responsibilities as you attempt to carve out time to prepare for the future.

It may also be that the school which you are leaving and the school to which you are moving are geographically distant, as was the case with a number of my research participants, so visits were not necessarily easy to manage and travelling was time consuming. Again, drawing up a plan for the whole of the lead-in period should enable you to make the most effective use of the time you have. If you are moving home and relocating your family (including finding new schools for your children), this is, of course, all a critical part of the plan.

It is well worth giving careful thought to what you might need to focus on in the lead-in phase, and, for this, I would go back to your very early research into the school and the role and your preparation for the application and interview process. Remind yourself of what you already know about the school and how, in terms of your temperament, skills, experiences and achievements so far, you are well placed to fill the role of the head. Then, crucially, identify where the gaps are, what you need to consolidate your learning about and consider how best you can do this before you formally assume the position.

Much of the learning may take place in visits to the new school and meetings with members of the school community, both on and off site. But there may also be much you can learn from staff you are working with in the school where you are a deputy, including the head. You may also have contacts external to both schools – for example, former colleagues, friends or contacts outside education – who can help you to build your skills and your confidence with respect to those areas in which you recognise your expertise is still developing. The important thing now is clearly to identify those areas.

Considering the experiences of my six research participants, the aspects of headship in which they sought to strengthen their knowledge and understanding in the lead-in period are as follows. Check the list and identify any elements which might also be pertinent to your situation. Then give thought to what you might add to the list and where you could source the information and specialist knowledge you need.

- Finance. My participants began by identifying which aspects of finance they were likely to be presented with in headship that might constitute an additional challenge. Spending time with the school business manager in their current schools – including working through, in confidence, financial information from the school they were joining – was one strategy my research participants used. Similarly, meeting with the finance director/chief accountant of the trust within which their current school was a member was productive. Some completed additional professional development courses on finance. Others ensured that they completed reading recommended by the finance professionals with whom they were in contact. The summer break after they had finished as deputies offered a useful opportunity to complete such reading – once they'd had a proper holiday and a much needed rest.

- Governance. Some deputies have significant experience of working with governors; others have considerably less contact with the governing body. If they were in the latter group, my participants asked to attend (perhaps simply as observers) governors' meetings (full governor and subcommittee meetings) just to listen, familiarise themselves with protocols and processes and learn. (My strong advice to senior leaders considering headship is to explore the possibility of joining the governing body of another school – perhaps a school of a different type – which will build knowledge and understanding of the head/ governor dynamic in a very helpful way.)

- Boarding. One of my participants moved to a school with boarding, having only previously had experience of day schools. Knowledge of such unfamiliar areas can be built during the lead-in period through contact with others with the relevant experience, perhaps including shadowing and observation. Careful thought needs to be given to what you think you need to know and where you might access that information. But be aware, also, that there will be 'unknown unknowns' at this stage.

- Early Years. One participant was taking over as head of a 3–11 school when her experience was primarily at Key Stage 2. As with boarding, time spent with Early Years specialists, including shadowing and observation, enabled her to begin to build her understanding and confidence in this area.

- Marketing and admissions. My participants all recognised that a greater proportion of their time might be spent on promoting the school, including to prospective families and students, and, in the light of this, learning from marketing and admissions professionals during the lead-in period was a productive use of their time. Some embarked on additional areas of activity in their current role to give them experience of a fuller contribution to the marketing and admissions elements of school life and a taste of what they might need to, or wish to, do in their headship capacity.

- Capital building projects. One of my participants had the opportunity to be involved in putting together a business case for a capital development project in the school where she was a deputy, including liaising with architects, and throughout this experience she was mindful of the opportunity it offered her to extend her learning in an area which might be relevant to her future responsibility as head.

- Safeguarding/child protection. Several of my research participants completed additional training in this area during the lead-in period, in one case alongside other senior staff in the school she was joining, which also gave her the opportunity to begin to build relationships with members of her new school community.

In addition to the specific areas above, which my six heads-elect had identified as elements of school leadership or aspects of school life in which they wished to strengthen their expertise, in all their day-to-day activities as deputies during the lead-in period they were conscious that they were beginning to view things from the perspective of the head. The most supportive heads my participants worked with as deputies were particularly adept at helping them to continue to develop their learning and preparation, especially with respect to some of the difficult decisions they might face in their headship role. A sensitive child protection case, staff disciplinary and capability processes, an official parental complaint which required the convening of a formal appeal panel and a tragic bereavement all offered these heads-elect the opportunity further to reflect on the decisions they might make and the actions they would take were they in the head's chair.

So, identify those aspects of school leadership in which you feel you need to build your knowledge or your confidence, and systematically search out sources of guidance and information. In addition, be mindful of any opportunities to consolidate your learning – and, in particular, your appreciation of the head's perspective – from the challenges which emerge in your current school during this period. Set aside some time to read and search out recommendations of useful texts – see, for example, the recommendations for further reading about leadership at the end of this book. Seek out further professional development in those areas where you consider you require it.

Perhaps look for online training, which has the advantage of being flexible and which you can usually complete asynchronously at a time to suit you, and therefore does not require further days out of school.[1]

The challenges of the lead-in period, and sources of support and strategies

Inevitably, the lead-in period will not be without its challenges, so in this section I shall explore what they might be and then outline some of the sources of support you might access, in addition to the strategies you can mobilise yourself, to help you meet them.

The first area of potential difficulty is to do with relationships. I have already discussed negotiating your relationship with the head you are succeeding, which can be one of the key challenges you face, if they themselves are finding their own transition difficult. Establishing the most positive relationships with all those members of your new school community with whom you come into contact during this time is another challenge. You may not have a great deal of time with them, and yet you need to ensure that the initial impressions you make are good ones – you are constantly being watched and evaluated and you need to be fully aware of this. Think carefully before you speak and be wary of the throw-away comment. Recognise that you may never be able to make a casual, half-thought-through comment in a professional context for the rest of

---

1   For example, Andrew Hampton, a serving independent school head, and I run a four-week online course on leading an independent school, during which we cover vision and values, marketing, finance, governance and leading the school through an inspection. Further details are available at: www.leadinganindependentschool.co.uk.

your career! You are the head now (or you soon will be). People will hang on your words, and they will sometimes misinterpret, repeat inaccurately or distort (not necessarily wilfully) what you say and interpret/extrapolate in ways you cannot easily anticipate. One of my participants discovered that something she had said during the lead-in period (when she was 'just thinking aloud') had subsequently caused her senior leaders sleepless nights!

In addition to building relationships with staff of all types – including the senior team and teaching and support staff – and with governors, you are likely also to have early opportunities to meet groups of pupils, parents, prospective parents and members of the wider community, perhaps including those schools which feed into your school or into which your school feeds. Again, you will be being judged, so you need to feel comfortable with that concept. You may at times be pushed to articulate your vision and future plans for the school. Although you will be starting to formulate such ideas, my strong advice would be to remain circumspect about what you say, and certainly what you promise, at this stage. You are not yet properly in post (and, even when you are, beware of making pronouncements too early). It would perhaps be presumptuous to make declarations and to state intentions clearly before you are actually in the role. In any case, any plans for the future are plans you will formalise alongside your governors and other staff, rather than schemes you will impose. You need to work with and through other staff to make such ideas a reality, and this requires their contribution, involvement and commitment. Similarly, you will inherit a vision (more of this in the next chapter) rather than import one – the vision will evolve – so I would be very careful about categorically stating how you will transform the school whose leadership you have assumed.

It may be that there is a member of the senior team, or even more than one, who unsuccessfully applied for the headship, and they will be dealing with their own disappointment. Four of my six participants were in this position. The attitude of the senior leader concerned is, as with your predecessor, something you need to address, but it is not something you can fully control. In the case of my participants, one unsuccessful deputy had already found another headship before the new head joined and she was moving on at the end of his first year. She was positive and supportive throughout his lead-in period and first year, her final year as deputy (during which she was managing her own lead-in period, of course). In another case, the disappointed deputy was professional and positive in their support of the incoming head (and he, too, secured a headship of his own within a couple of years). In the two other cases, the unsuccessful internal headship candidates were bruised and sensitive; it may not have been the 'fault' of the incoming head that they themselves had not been selected, but it definitely coloured their relationship with the successful appointee and there were tensions that had to be navigated. Interestingly, neither of these colleagues had applied for a headship before (see the section in Chapter 2 on applying for headship as an internal candidate if you have never before expressed an interest in moving to be a head).

If you judge that the unsuccessful internal candidate is capable of securing a headship of their own in a different school, then my advice would be to articulate your commitment to supporting them to do so, and to ensure you fulfil this commitment. They may be a strong senior leader whom you are sorry to see leave but, just as you will have been supported earlier in your career, investing in the professional development of talented future leaders will be an important part of your role as a head. Help to prepare this aspiring head for making the transition, just as you are now doing.

If, however, you consider that the disappointed senior leader is not suited to headship, or certainly not yet, then you will need to be sensitive and help them to see this over time. By doing a conscientious and committed job yourself you should be able to earn their respect. If they have sufficient self-awareness you may be able to support them to see that, although they felt they were a credible candidate for the role of school leader, they do not yet have the required skills to make a success of headship. Guiding them to be the best they can be in their current role, and ensuring they find satisfaction and reward in that position, will be crucial. If the relationship continues to be problematic, seeking the counsel of your governing body would be wise – the governors will know this senior colleague far better than you do at this stage. Stress that you do not expect the governing body to deal with the situation, but you are seeking their advice as you attempt to resolve any tension.

If the outgoing head was particularly successful, or especially popular, then the challenge for the head-elect of building positive relationships with all groups within the school community from the outset can be particularly acute. Hargreaves and Fink (2006: 92) describe 'the Rebecca myth (from Daphne du Maurier's novel *Rebecca*, that the predecessor was an irreplaceable paragon of virtue)', and there may be times when an incoming head feels like the narrator in this novel who believes she will never measure up in the light of this competition (until she discovers, of course, that the reality was rather different). The issue here is fundamentally one of confidence and self-belief. I will explore this more fully, and how the difficulty can be addressed, in the next chapter when I discuss the tension between inheriting and inhabiting the role.

The head-elect may also find that balancing competing priorities tests them. You are still carrying out a demanding deputy role, to which you will be (and certainly should be) committed to fulfilling conscientiously and thoroughly until the end of your time in the school – which may be late August if you are starting your headship in the autumn term. Your deputy job will always have been time consuming and demanding. In addition to this you are now beginning to be pulled towards your new school and impending role – certainly in terms of your preoccupations and mental energy, even if you are physically present in your current school. Your present school is where your loyalty should lie, but as the lead-in period progresses you may find that your head is in a different place and your thoughts are increasingly taken up with what lies in the future – and that is becoming imminent.

If you are being replaced as a deputy, which is the norm, you may also be called upon to support the process with respect to the appointment of your successor (although, as with the situation of your predecessor in the school to which you are moving, as the outgoing incumbent you are unlikely to have an active role in the actual selection process). Once this appointment is made, however, you will need to spend time helping your successor to make a positive transition to their new role. You should help to prepare them, as you yourself are preparing to take on your next role. You will be building a bridge between your time in the deputy post and theirs, ensuring continuity and coherence for the sake of the school you are leaving.

If your successor is internally appointed this can have advantages – they are already in the school, so communication and liaison with them may be easier than when an externally appointed deputy visits the school in blocks of time when you have to prioritise contact with them. However, as with the situation of the internally appointed head candidate discussed earlier in this chapter, outgoing deputies whose successors are internally appointed can begin to feel uncomfortable and supplanted too early. One of my research participants whose successor as deputy was already in the school talked to me of how 'you lose an element of authority quite quickly'. He described himself as feeling like 'yesterday's man on the slow march to the door'. If this is the case, a frank (though calm and professional) conversation with the head of the school may be in order.

The difficulty of balancing competing priorities can be exacerbated if the school to which you are moving as head begins to make early demands on you, expecting you to spend more time, thought and energy on what is happening at that school, or on what is proposed for the future, than you feel you can currently devote to it. You may be wary of taking decisions, the repercussions of which you cannot fully anticipate (or subsequently mitigate), as you are not yet in post. Balance involvement in the life of your new school so that you start to know and be known, without having to commit to so much involvement that you feel you are taking on too much too early.

This relates to the third area of challenge in the lead-in period, which is that of pacing yourself and your energies through this time. My six research participants found that information and demands, plus the expectations they were placing on themselves with respect to taking on the headship, were coming at them thick and fast throughout the lead-in period. As the time passed, their brains were getting fuller. They were keen to ensure that they kept control of the information, their thoughts and ideas at this early stage, so that they did not forget or overlook crucial things, that they had a sense of the big picture, but that they were not overwhelmed or intimidated by this, especially as they were at the same time managing their current challenging day job.

The priority was pacing themselves throughout the lead-in period, making the most of opportunities to learn, while keeping a sense of clarity and proportion. Experience of their new school's context and growing familiarity with its personnel and systems were enabling them to confirm and consolidate initial impressions. As time passed, and the lead-in period drew to an end (and the point where they would formally assume their new role loomed large), their knowledge was growing. The challenge was keeping a secure grasp on this so that they could take full advantage of their increasing understanding.

Having identified three specific areas of challenge in the lead-in period – building relationships, balancing competing priorities and pacing their energies – in the rest of this chapter I shall explore three potential channels of support and three specific strategies my participants used to help them as they faced these challenges in the months prior to taking up their headship.

The first source of support, not only during the lead-in period but throughout your headship, relates to the networks you are able to construct. It is often said that headship is lonely; I didn't find it lonely, mainly owing to the personal and professional networks I could draw on for support, energy and sustenance of different kinds. Consider the networks you already have, including role models, mentors and coaches from your career thus far, and how you can continue to build and strengthen such networks. You may find you use different networks for different purposes.

In terms of personal networks, family and friends beyond education can be extremely important if you are not to feel isolated and vulnerable in headship. Creating a sustainable balance between your personal and professional responsibilities and relationships is crucial. Know when to switch off, including literally, by disconnecting from the devices which attach you to your professional role. Through your interests beyond your job (and, no matter how committed, conscientious and professionally driven you are, I would insist that this is your job, and not your life), you need to continue to find ways to relax and unwind. If it is not possible to do a good job and have a life, I would maintain that there is something wrong with the job, not with you. So find opportunities to rest, refresh and re-energise, including at weekends and in the holidays, so that you return to school with renewed energy, ready to face the challenges the coming weeks will bring.

Make use, too, of professional networks. You may belong to a group of fellow new heads, who are likely to understand the process of transition you are going through better than anyone else, as they are all at a similar point in their professional journey. Sometimes these are colleagues you have met through formal preparation programmes, such as the NPQH, or through new heads' induction programmes. Use them as sounding boards, in confidence, during the lead-in period if you are addressing particular issues. Learn from them and benefit from their experience.

You may be in a regional or cluster group which can be another source of guidance and support. You may use social networking for educational professional development – I am a huge fan of Twitter and the world of blogging to create a personal/professional learning network which is customised to your specific needs.[2]

There may be other groups, including former colleagues who have moved on to headship perhaps a few years ahead of you, on whom you can draw for wise counsel or even just a listening ear. Often you do not need anyone to tell you what to do – you already know what you should do – but talking it through with someone who understands and who wishes you well can help to clarify your thinking and to articulate what action you should take.

In addition to networks, consider the significant role models who have inspired, motivated and encouraged you so far, and how you may be able to make use of their expertise and judgement as mentors or coaches throughout the lead-in period and beyond. The head of the school where you are currently a deputy may be one such positive model. You may be moving to a school or trust, or be a

---

2   See Jefferis (2016) for an analysis of the use of Twitter for head teachers' professional development.

member of a professional association, which is prepared to invest in mentoring or coaching for you. If a formal mentoring or coaching arrangement is not offered, this may well be worth discussing with your governing body. Any governing body worth its salt should recognise that the job is not 'done' because the head is appointed. All incoming leaders, in any field, will need ongoing, flexible, negotiated, targeted support and training if they are to fulfil their leadership potential. Mentors and coaches can be extremely helpful here.

The second source of support comes from the school community you are joining. This includes the governing body/ trust that has appointed you, has confidence in you and is invested in your success, and the senior team with whom you will work closely. You need to build the most positive and constructive relationships with the members of this school community. As you face the challenges of the lead-in period, you are not alone. Make the best use of the expertise and understanding of the school, which is shared by those within it, as you consolidate your learning and build your confidence with respect to this new context. If you are able to establish a good relationship with your predecessor, this will be part of the support. Where the senior team is concerned, get to know them individually and tune in to their complementary skills, considering how you can best utilise these skills to support you as you progress through the lead-in period and prepare to take up the role.

If you are an externally appointed head, you will not yet know the people, systems, policies and processes within your new school, but your established senior team will. By working with and through them you will continue to build your knowledge and understanding, but also clearly demonstrate that your senior team has a crucial contribution to make to the continuing development and success of the school. Showing your awareness and appreciation of this can also support the building of the most positive relationships with your new senior team members.

Working alongside your new governing body will also be key. Revisiting the school's vision and values, and considering priority areas for further development, is a process which is likely to begin in the months before you formally take up the post. Governors will have a range of expertise which you will make the most of during your time as head. Establishing a mutually respectful relationship with the governors can support and strengthen you during the lead-in time and help you to manage other relationships, as well as the challenges of prioritisation and pacing which this stage of transition may present.

The final source of support to consider relates to any external agencies you can draw on for additional guidance. I have already mentioned professional associations – such as, for incoming heads in the independent sector, the Headmasters' and Headmistresses' Conference (HMC) and Girls' Schools Association (GSA). Consider also your union – for example, the Association of School and College Leaders (ASCL) or National Association of Head Teachers (NAHT) – and bodies such as the National College for Teaching and Leadership (NCTL). Such organisations offer advisers, helplines or membership secretaries whose role is to support professionals, and who have access to expertise and resources which you may be able to draw on if any particular elements of the lead-in period are causing you concern.

In addition to these three channels of support, there will also be strategies you yourself devise which can help you to make the most of the lead-in time.

The first of these is careful planning. As discussed, the lead-in time can be potentially overwhelming as you balance your current professional responsibilities as deputy and prepare for your future role as head. You will find information and ideas coming thick and fast. You need to pace yourself and to be reasonably methodical and systematic about how you deal with this so that you do not feel inundated and out of control. Consider the following and whether these tactics might work for you:

- A familiarisation plan, which includes a timeline/ calendar of key events and commitments and which clearly identifies priorities for what you need to learn and achieve during the lead-in period, can help you to pace yourself successfully.

- Decide what you need to do now, what you could leave for the holiday immediately prior to taking up the role, what you need to do at the start of term (in the first week, the first month), what can be left for the first major holiday after your first term and so on. Write it down and keep it safe. The list will evolve and change over time – edit it and adapt it as necessary – but keeping a written record can help you to keep track of what the priorities are and ensure that you do not neglect or forget things which occur to you which may not be imminent but which will need addressing at some point in the future.

- Work backwards from key deadlines. If there are things you need to read, to draft or to plan (e.g. your leaving speech in your current school, your first staff meeting in your new school, your first assembly, your first governors' meeting), decide when you will tackle each task to give yourself sufficient time to do it well (and I would suggest that in addition to planning a speech, staff address or an initial assembly, you may need to practise it, too). If you diarise such tasks it can help you to manage inevitable feelings of nervousness about them. At least you are allocating sufficient time so that you will be well prepared.

The second strategy which can support you during the lead-in period is ensuring that you are sufficiently receptive and responsive to feedback, and that you learn from experience. You will certainly have your own ideas, a sense of your own vision and values, and a clearly developed educational philosophy which you have honed over time – and on the strength of which you were no doubt appointed to the headship. However, although your principles may be firm, in my view sensitivity to context and the capacity to adapt and be flexible in your thinking are key to success in leadership.

Your skills and understanding will continue to build as a result of these things: visits to the school, meetings with key constituents of the school community, reading, reflection and further learning about different aspects of headship from colleagues on whose expertise you are drawing. You will need to be prepared to challenge some of your assumptions and preconceptions, to examine your role expectations where headship is concerned, and to recognise that there may be conflicting role expectations held by different members of the school you are joining which will have an impact on how you enact the role.

As I discovered from my research, when the head of a school changes, this is not simply about the journey of one person. The process of socialisation, as a new head adjusts to a new school community (or, if internally promoted, adjusts to a new role within a known school community), is two-way. I shall discuss this more fully in the next chapter, but in terms of the strategies heads-elect can adopt to make the fullest and most productive use of the lead-in period, and to navigate its potential challenges, I would suggest that receptivity to feedback and learning from experience are key.

Finally, the third strategy which incoming heads can mobilise as they face the demands of the lead-in period is a reliance on their inner resources and strength. Having faith in your own capacity and confidence in your ability to adapt, to grow and to learn will take you a long way. Remember, you have been appointed by the selection panel in this particular school because, not only did they feel you were capable of doing the job, and doing it well, but they were also convinced you were capable of doing it *better* than any other contender. You will, of course, not know everything about headship or be able to fulfil the role of head perfectly from the outset (or ever?). But the fact that you have been appointed is recognition that those who know the school well – and much better than you do at this point – are convinced that you are a good match for what the school needs at this stage of its journey. Don't forget, you will build the bridge as you walk on it.

As you face the challenges of the lead-in period – building relationships, including with the outgoing head; consolidating your learning, both professional (the demands of headship) and organisational (the characteristics and priorities of this particular school at this point); balancing your demanding deputy head commitments while finding time to prepare for the future; pacing yourself and planning your way through a very busy period of your professional life – you also have the opportunity to show your mettle. The things which test us also offer us a valuable opportunity to prove ourselves – to ourselves as well as to others. As you rise to a challenge, you develop your capacity to cope with it. And you are beginning to create the space within which you can make your mark, do the job in a way which is true to you and which satisfies your conception of what the best school leadership looks like – a conception you will have formulated and refined throughout your career. You will have learnt from positive, inspiring role models. You will have learnt from leaders you felt were less successful. You now have the opportunity to go on to emulate the best and be better than the negative leader role models you have known. This is a challenge, certainly, but it is also a privilege and a tremendous opportunity.

Your inner resources are what you will draw on in the years and months ahead: your conviction, commitment, determination to do the job well and to make it your own. You want to leave the school better than you found it – no matter how strong and successful it might currently be. The next chapter covers how you might begin to do this in the early months in post.

Questions for reflection

- If you are embarking on the lead-in period following successful appointment to headship, consider the specific context of the school you are to join. Identify any areas in which you could build your expertise before officially taking up the post.

- Where will you go for support as you develop these areas, and how can you continue to construct and strengthen your networks?

- Is there any early indication of how positive, or how taxing, your relationship with your predecessor is likely to be? What strategies can you adopt to establish mutual understanding and support?

- Will you draw up a familiarisation plan and, if so, at what stage and who should be involved?

- How might you address the situation if you believe you are (a) kept uncomfortably at arm's length or (b) overly consulted and involved in the life of the school you are joining?

- If you have been internally appointed, what pitfalls can you identify and how can you avoid them? What advantages do you have and how can you make the most of them?

- If you are externally appointed, how can you accelerate your learning at this time?

- What can you do to support your successor to the deputy role?

Chapter 4

The early months in post

'Inheriting' the role versus 'inhabiting' the role

Inevitably, when you take over as head, you aren't inheriting a blank canvas on which to write as you wish. By this stage, it will be clear to you from the research you carried out prior to applying, from the preparation you did before interview and from your learning during the lead-in period that you are stepping into a role which your predecessor (and the heads who went before them) has made their own. To a certain extent, the expectations of the different members of the school community, and of the wider community within which the school sits, will have an impact on how you are able to enact the role. It is important to respect the contributions of those who went before, to recognise that there are customs and traditions in which those you will lead may be strongly invested, and that when you are making changes you may appear retrospectively critical of the heads who preceded you, and this can make others – for example, your senior team – feel uncomfortable and even disloyal.

However, any new head will want to put their own stamp on the role and to make their mark. In this way they are not content with 'inheriting' the role, but they also want to 'inhabit' it, and to leave the school better than they found it. This tension between inheriting and inhabiting relates to the concept of reciprocal socialisation. As the incoming head adapts to their new professional practice and identity, they will change the community they join. However, the community will also change the head in some ways, so the head is not the only one who is undergoing a process of socialisation. Incoming heads will need to be sensitive to context, to tune in to the norms, the perceptions, the passions and the insecurities of others. You should not ride roughshod over their feelings. However, you will also need to be true to yourself, your vision and values, your principles and priorities. You will want and need to assert yourself, to lead the school in your own way and not to be constrained by the way in which those who went before fulfilled the role of head.

So how do you do this? In this chapter I shall draw on my own experiences, my reading and my research to suggest ways in which you might establish yourself as positively as you can in the early months. There will be some practical ideas you may wish to use, and certainly some elements of being a new head which you will need to reflect on. However, there is no blueprint for success and no single way of getting this right. Much will depend on the individual context of the school, your own skills and temperament, and the response of others both during your lead-in period and in your first term. As Despontin (2007: 15) states: 'There *is* only one way to be a Head, and that is your way.'

Matthews and Crow (2003) describe the difference between 'role-taking' and 'role-making'. In their view, heads who take over successful, well-led schools are likely to focus on role-taking – stepping into the shoes of the outgoing head without causing too much of a stir and focussing on maintaining current standards. They suggest that heads who take over in more difficult circumstances, including perhaps succeeding a weaker leader, may find themselves invested in role-making – having to make significant change and shape more proactively how the role of head is enacted.

On the basis of my six research participants' experiences, I would propose that this is too simplistic, and that the transition to new headship is a more complex and nuanced process. All of the six incoming heads took over in schools that were, to some degree, successful, and from heads who were, in the main, effective and respected. However, I would assert that all six recognised they were different from their predecessors in a number of ways, and they were determined to inhabit this role and not just to inherit it. All were keen to make the job, and the school during the time of their tenure, their own. Generally, they did so thoughtfully and sensitively; they recognised that they had to take their time over some things, and perhaps to work initially to put structures and systems in place which would enable them to lead as they felt they should. But they were all making the role, rather than simply taking the role.

Learning to lead in a new context

So, you have been honing your leadership skills throughout your career so far, perhaps even before your career in education began, and learning about leadership from role models, positive and negative, along the way. You may have formulated clear ideas about the leader you hope to be, although you know that this is something you will have to work towards, and this leader will not emerge, butterfly-like, from the chrysalis of the lead-in period on the day you officially step into the role. This perfect leader may, in fact, never emerge, and you may find that your perception of what this leader is like changes over time. There is the leader you most want to be. There is the leader this particular school requires you to be at this stage in its development – and, of course, at later stages, as time passes and your experience, confidence and competence grow alongside the school's changing needs. And there is also the leader the school will allow you to be, and you may be acutely aware of this, especially in the early months.

If you have been sufficiently discriminating in your choice of school, and are comfortable that this is a school which is to some degree aligned with what you stand for as an educationalist and as a leader, any initial mismatch between how you would prefer to lead and how you are required to lead should not prove too problematic. To take an example from my research participants: it may be that you are very keen to empower others, to give them responsibility and to trust their judgement and their capacity to lead in their particular areas without too much interference from you. You may be committed to the principle of having the overview, as head, resisting micromanagement and what you consider to be too heavy-handed leadership. It may be that this is the leadership style you have been most impressed with in the past, and it sits well with your own skills and temperament. Perhaps at an earlier stage of your career you were given autonomy by the head and, as a keen and capable middle or senior leader, you thrived and grew because you were trusted and given the space to do a job in your own way.

However, as an incoming head, you may find that, although this is the ideal situation towards which you are working, you do not currently have the structure, or staff of a sufficiently high calibre, for this leadership style to work. You may find that you have to spend your early months in post trying to create the right structure and appoint the right people to the right roles in order for this to be how your new school eventually operates. Your current senior team, for example, was not selected by you, so there may be people in it whom you would never have chosen, or certainly not for the roles they have.

Probably the most common scenario is that there is a lack of consistency; some of those you lead are strong, others less so. Some are well suited to their roles, while others, for whatever reason, are in positions which do not comfortably align with their strengths. You will have been building your knowledge and understanding throughout the lead-in period, and now in your early months in the head's chair you have to learn how to lead in this particular context.

Consider the following three strategies:

1. Get to know the different members of the school community well. Your predecessor may have given

you information about some of them but that was his/her perception. Give them the benefit of the doubt and offer them the chance to prove themselves to you. Perhaps the fresh beginning your arrival heralds will help to bring out the best in them. It could be that they respond more positively to your leadership than they did to that of your predecessor. Don't be too quick to judge, especially to judge harshly.

2. Using the appreciative enquiry model (see page 53), consider where the strengths of the school are and what the different people you work with may be good at. Can you see the best in them in order to get the best from them? Can you catch them doing something right, rather than fixating anxiously on catching them doing something wrong? I believe everyone is good at something. Have you found it, and are you helping them to make use of it? If these strengths are not matched to their roles and responsibilities, think about the staffing structure you might want to move to over time and take initial steps towards that whenever and wherever the opportunity emerges.

3. If you have got to know staff well, and done your very best to focus on the positives, but you have serious concerns that there are key members of staff in important roles who are not able to do what they need to do for the school to function successfully, then this may be a nettle you need to grasp. Talk to the chair of governors in confidence and make use of their experience and insights. Go through proper channels so as not to find yourself on the wrong side of an employment tribunal, and always treat

staff with respect and humanity. But recognise that if someone is in a role for which they are simply not suited, then they are probably unhappy and frustrated. Your first recourse should always be to support staff to do the best job they can. You should not be too quick to leap to judgement and criticism, and capability processes are the last step in the journey, not one of the first. But if leading the school, realising its vision and enabling those within the school community to be their best is jeopardised by the staffing and structures you have inherited, then you need to have the courage to take some difficult decisions and make changes in due course.

How can you best get to know the staff well at an early stage in your tenure? These are some of the strategies I used as a new head. Consider whether they might work in your context.

As a newly appointed head, I saw each member of staff individually for an informal twenty-minute chat in my first term. This included all the teaching staff and a good number of support staff. To give a structure to our conversation, I asked them all to tell me one thing about the school which they would like to see changed and one thing they hoped would never change. I found it a very helpful way of taking the temperature of the school. It was revealing that in terms of what people wanted to change, there were a number of suggestions but relatively little consistency. I knew this was a successful school which had been skilfully led by my predecessor, and this response from the staff confirmed that. There might be some frustrations and minor irritations, but nothing major was causing widespread concern. However, when it came to the things the staff would not change, there was a great deal of consistency. Their answers gave me further insight into what the school was doing particularly well, what the members of the school community valued and what they were keen to preserve.

I remember the conversation with one member of staff, a part-time teacher who had worked at the school for eleven years and who was also the parent of a pupil. Before she told me what she wanted to change and to preserve, she took a deep breath and said, 'I just want to say that I've been here for eleven years and this is the first time I've had a one-to-one conversation with the head. It's also the first time anyone has asked me to tell them honestly what I think about the school.' After she had left I reflected that, for that comment alone and the message it conveyed, having these one-to-one meetings was going to be very well worth the time it would take.

From the beginning (and this had been a feature of my use of the lead-in period too), I made the decision to go to as many extra-curricular activities as I could possibly fit in. I did this because I thought it was a good way to get to know people (staff, pupils, parents, governors and members of the wider community) and to begin to be known. So I went to drama and music rehearsals, debates and public speaking events, sports fixtures, Young Enterprise competitions, Combined Cadet Force activities and Duke of Edinburgh's Award scheme expeditions, school trips, a huge range of clubs and activities, charity fundraising initiatives – anything I could manage. Chatting to parents on the sidelines of sports matches, for example, was pleasant and interesting, but also useful as I began to build my knowledge base and to establish the most positive personal relationships I could. It was good to see the staff in a range of contexts, too, and to appreciate (and for them to see I was appreciative of) the many ways in which they went above and beyond their contracted responsibilities to offer the pupils experiences and opportunities which they believed would enrich their education.

And it was hugely enjoyable. I felt a pride in the school and those who were part of it (now my school) so this wasn't simply a duty, it was a pleasure. In many respects, having done this at the outset of my tenure as head, it then simply became what I did – throughout my ten years there I went to a significant number of extra-curricular events; in fact, if I didn't go to something it was usually because I was already committed elsewhere. Because of the nature of my role there were times when I only managed to call in to an event for ten minutes. But I found that often people didn't mind that; they were just pleased I had shown an interest and been there. If I congratulated pupils afterwards for their contribution, and thanked the member of staff concerned for giving the pupils that opportunity, it meant more because I'd seen it. I'd been there.

So meeting the staff was a good way of starting to get to know them, and going to a significant number of events helped me to get to know them better and to interact with pupils and parents in a productive way. But what about the lessons? Teaching and learning are clearly key – this is our core purpose. Our pastoral provision is important because we care about our pupils and we do all we can to underpin and support their learning. Extra-curricular involvement, including showing a sense of social responsibility and supporting each other and those beyond the school, as was the case with much of the charity work the pupils engaged in, was important because this was all part of their wider learning – education in its broadest sense. But what happened in the classroom was at the centre of the life of the school, and to get to know the school well in the early months I needed to be in there to experience it.

I fully realised that, while a member of staff might be pleased if I called in to support the hockey match or the choir practice, they might be less keen if they found I was sitting at the back of their lesson. So I tackled this in two ways. First, I told the staff that I would be delighted if they wanted to invite me in to lessons to see any particular activity the pupils were involved in that they thought I would find interesting and where the pupils themselves would appreciate my interest. Several did – perhaps the most confident initially – and I was able to visit lessons without causing too much of a stir. It was good to have the opportunity to discuss the experience with the teacher afterwards. Next, in my second term, I carried out a pupil pursuit exercise, where I followed one pupil from each year group for a day, attending all their lessons. This was a 7–18 school so it took me eleven days to shadow one pupil in each of Years 3 to 13.

The heads of section chose the pupils, and I explained to pupils and staff that I was just interested in finding out more about the pupils' perspectives and typical experiences. I was focussing on their learning, rather than the teachers' 'performance', and this wasn't a judgemental exercise – I was there to learn, not to assess/grade. It was about encouraging reflection and opening a dialogue. I saw some teachers teach several times, while others I didn't see at all – it depended on the pupils the heads of section chose, the particular lessons they happened to have and the particular teachers they were taught by on the day I shadowed them.

After each lesson I made notes based on my reflections, ultimately feeding back at a whole-school staff meeting on what I had seen and learnt (positively) about what the experience of a pupil in this school, at different ages, might be like. It helped me to develop further insights. It helped me to continue to build relationships. Above all, it helped me to have a better understanding of the context within which I was leading.

Head teachers have to make a decision about whether they are going to teach themselves, and if so who and how it will be arranged. I would also suggest they need to consider why. In my view, it shouldn't be for selfish reasons. If we teach simply because we enjoy teaching and don't want to give it up, then we need to think this through carefully. We are now the highest paid member of staff. We need to be good, credible teachers, but we may not be the best teachers in the school. We don't have to be – that isn't our job. Our job is to do all we can to ensure that all the other teachers in the school are the best they can be. And I also don't think we should use the classroom as an escape. We may be well within our comfort zone there – we are in control, we know our subject and our capacity to communicate our understanding and enthusiasm to young people. But if there are other, demanding tasks outside the classroom door waiting for the head's attention – tasks which, actually, only the head should do – then sheltering behind the classroom door can be self-indulgent and a distraction.

We also need to ask ourselves whether the classes taught by the head will get the best deal, especially if we find, because of the nature of our job, that we are more frequently out of school than other teachers, so the lessons are disrupted. Is it fair to teach in these circumstances?

Eight years before I was appointed as a head, I was interviewed for a deputy head post. I was 33 and in my eleventh year of teaching. The post was advertised as a non-teaching role. I applied and was invited for interview, and managed to get through to the second round of interviews and the final four candidates. At that stage, in an interview with the head and other senior staff, I was invited to ask questions, and my question was: why is this a non-teaching role? I felt I would be capable of fulfilling the post while still doing some teaching. In fact, I thought that teaching would help me to do the job well – this was a new school so not somewhere I had taught already. I tried to explain how I believed teaching would give me more credibility, would help me to understand the school's systems and processes, and would enable me to build better relationships with pupils. The head listened and then said, quite sharply, 'You wouldn't have time to teach.' I didn't get the job. I was disappointed, as I'd liked the school, but I wasn't confident that the head and I would have worked well together.

When I became a head, I realised it was *my* choice whether I taught or not – this wasn't something the governors or anyone else would dictate. But I thought that if I did decide to teach, I would have to consider who I would teach, how it would be arranged and, crucially, why I was choosing to do so and how the pupils I taught would be affected. Was it self-indulgent, an escape and potentially detrimental to the classes who happened to be timetabled to be taught by me?

I did teach, and I taught for each of the ten years I was there. I taught one English lesson each week to each of the Year 7 classes – usually four, but occasionally five, classes in this year group. I was paired with their 'usual' English teacher, so if I had to be out of school the class was taught English as normal and they wouldn't suffer. When I was in school, I wouldn't schedule anything to interfere with my lessons – they were sacrosanct.

So why did I do it? I did it to get to know the individual pupils as soon as possible. By October half term I knew the names of all those in Year 7. If pupils joined us in Years 8, 9, 10 or 12, these were in smaller numbers and I got to know them through the admissions process, so it wasn't a problem that I hadn't taught them. By the time I had been in the school for seven years, I knew each pupil in the senior school. I was the only member of staff fortunate enough to be able to do that, and it was invaluable. When pupils came up in assembly to be presented with certificates and medals, I never had to ask who was who and I never gave the wrong one to the wrong child. It reflected and reinforced our commitment to valuing each individual.

I didn't know each individual pupil in the junior school section of the school, though I knew an increasing number as time passed. However, the head of juniors did. She ensured that she taught all new classes so there was one key member of staff in that section of the school who could confidently address each pupil by name. If you claim that the individual is important, and that you are attempting to personalise their learning to the best of your ability, then this is one way in which the way you operate day to day can reinforce that stated commitment.

Of course, if you are internally appointed to your headship you will already know many members of the school community and you will already understand the school's context. You will have a well-developed sense of its journey so far, and you may have formulated a clear view of where you think it should be going, and how it might get there, over your years as a deputy.

What will change, however, is your position within that landscape. Although you will be building on established relationships and on your current role within the school community, nevertheless, the dynamic will change when you step up to the headship. While still remaining true to yourself, your values and your principles, you will find that moving to headship requires a significant shift. Your role has changed and so will your focus and priorities. The evolution of your professional persona is something to which both you, and the school community which already knows you well, will need to adapt. This is the focus of the next section of this chapter.

Navigating the differences between deputy headship and headship

Whether you are internally or externally appointed to headship, one of the things you will need to address is the difference between the professional identity of the deputy and that of the head. You will want to fulfil the role in a way which is consistent with your educational philosophy and your vision and values as a leader. You cannot and should not try to become a different person when you move into the head's office. This is not about seeing yourself as more important than you were or suddenly better than those you lead. As one of my research participants put it:

> I made the decision to carry on being me ... I respect the role very much and expect other people to respect the role, but I still – if the tea needs pouring I'll pour the tea! Because I used to do that. I don't see why I should stop just because I'm a head.

However, you do need to recognise that there are key differences between your role as a deputy and the role of the head. You have to make a significant adjustment. If you are internally promoted, the school community of which you are already a member also needs to adjust the way in which they see you.

One internally appointed head I know said:

> Things started to go wrong when I interfered with tasks and responsibilities I had fulfilled as a deputy there – when I thought, 'Oh, I can just sort that out myself.' I couldn't, and it wasn't my job any more.

Some of the comments made by my externally appointed research participants are pertinent here. One said, in advance of formally stepping into the head's role:

> As a deputy I've been fully involved in the day-to-day life of the school. One challenge I anticipate may be moving out of that role and, I suppose, letting other people do it.

And another, after their first few months in post:

> When I was a deputy I organised everything ... Now I'm a head it's been a case of realising – trust your deputy, she's able to do it, let her get on with it.

So what are the key differences between the role of the deputy and the role of the head?

What follows are, inevitably, generalisations which will not be true of all deputies or all heads. Deputy roles, in particular, vary significantly. How well your deputy headship has given you a taste of, and prepared you for taking on, the role of the school leader will depend on a number of factors. It depends on whether the head you have served as a deputy has been invested in helping you ready yourself for the move to headship – sharing things, coaching you and encouraging you to consider, 'What would *you* do if …?' It depends on how far-reaching your deputy role has been and whether you are the sole deputy, or the senior deputy, who has, in effect, taken the place of the head when the head is absent from school. You may even have had an extended period as acting head if circumstances have required it – an excellent opportunity to hone your school leader skills. It also depends on your temperament to some degree and how proactive you have been in seeking out chances to develop your range of skills, venturing into new areas of responsibility, perhaps facing particularly tough challenges which have taken you well out of your comfort zone but which have stretched you and enabled you to grow.

However well prepared you are, and however well informed and aware you may consider yourself to be with respect to the differences you will face when you take on the head's role, it is only by actually experiencing it that you can fully understand the nature of the responsibility that you have assumed. As one of my research participants put it, a term into headship:

> When you have your first child, nobody really tells you what it's like to take on that responsibility as a parent. You have to have gone through it yourself. That's what it's like to become a head. Suddenly it's yours. You are responsible. You have to make the decisions. And it was actually humbling to have a chance to make those decisions.

On the one hand, being a deputy is the best preparation for moving to headship, for all the reasons outlined in earlier chapters. On the other hand, the focus of the role is quite different.

Although deputies should be involved in strategy and ideally have a well-developed relationship with the governing body, including perhaps the opportunity to present to governors on key issues, nevertheless, their day-to-day priorities are often operational. Deputies keep things running smoothly – addressing issues, finding solutions to problems, dealing with conflict. This may be conflict between pupils, between pupils and staff, between staff members, between staff and parents, and sometimes between the staff and the head. Deputies find a way forward.

This can mean that deputies find they are often reactive. As a deputy, I remember driving into work and wondering what that day might hold. It would depend on which child had a meltdown, which members of staff sought me out, the tone and content of the emails I received, which parent was on the telephone, perhaps even on the mood of the head! I remember how disconcerting I found this initially; I am an organised person who likes to plan ahead. I realised I still had to be systematic and well prepared so that, whatever claimed my time – and barring the very serious unexpected challenge – I could teach my lessons, honour my scheduled meeting sessions, lead an assembly, deal with the cover arrangements and the daily bulletin. I soon acclimatised to the firefighter elements of my deputy head role and came to enjoy the challenge of dealing with the unanticipated without it derailing me and preventing me from fulfilling my more routine responsibilities to the best of my ability. I liked the fact that I had to think on my feet, use my judgement, interact with a wide range of different people and know when I had the autonomy to take action, when I needed to ensure I informed the head of the action I had taken and when I needed to seek the head's counsel before I acted.

As a deputy, and I was the sole deputy in a 4–18 school of 1,100 pupils, I felt I knew how everything worked. Certainly, by my fifth year in the school I had a confident knowledge and general understanding of the people, systems and policies. When anyone came to me for information and advice, I felt comfortable that if I didn't know the answer, I would know where to go to find it. For me, being a deputy involved having a finger in every pie.

However, as a deputy your autonomy is inevitably limited. It helps if you have a trusting and mutually respectful relationship with your head and governing body, so you do not feel you have to ask permission for much of what you do and the decisions you take. Even so, you are the deputy and not the head.

This is, of course, part of the appeal of wanting to move to headship – because you want to extend your sphere of influence and have the status and the power to take bigger decisions and have a greater impact on the school as a whole. When reflecting on their current roles as deputies and their motivation for applying for headship, two of my research participants said:

> In my current role as deputy I'm reaching the limits of what I can do to make a whole-school difference, and I want to move on before I become stale or bored.

> The fundamental thing is that you can really change things when you're a head in a way you can't so much as a deputy. To actually be the initiator and to allow those things then to flow is a very exciting prospect.

Each felt they had reached a kind of plateau in their deputy role and they were concerned that, without the fresh challenge that moving to headship would bring, they might become professionally less engaged or less effective.

So navigating the difference between the professional identity of deputy and head is an important part of the appeal of moving to headship. Being the one to whom others defer, rather than the one you are standing behind, may bring trepidation, but it also brings excitement, energy and a rush of adrenaline which powers you through the early weeks and months in the role. Suddenly there is no safety net. This inevitably brings with it mixed feelings, as one of my participants observed:

> Ultimately everything I do as a deputy, there is always a safety blanket, and in some ways I'm looking forward to having the buck stop with me, scary though that is on occasions.

When you're a head people look to you for leadership. They look to you for a steer, a clear sense of direction. The new heads whose progress I followed all started by re-examining the vision of the schools they had moved to to lead. When the head changes it is an apposite time to revisit what the school stands for and how well that is articulated, understood and communicated both within and beyond the school community. New heads do not import their own vision, although they will have been appointed partly on the strength of their personal values and educational philosophy, so this will play an important part in the evolution of the school's ethos. But the head, working closely with the governing body and the senior team, and in consultation with all the teaching and support staff, pupils and parents, will be the one to drive and facilitate the process.

As a new head I remember leading such a consultation process in connection with the revision of our school's strategic plan, then collating all the information which had been generated and attempting to synthesise it into a reasonably concise statement, which was coherent and accurately summed up what made the school distinctive and how we could be differentiated from other schools. This statement had to align with how we actually operated: it had to make sense to those who worked within the school and who knew it well. There needed to be a clear connection between the rhetoric and the reality. I also wanted to be able to condense our statement of vision and values into one pithy phrase which would be memorable and which governors, staff, parents and pupils could buy into and use. We chose 'Discover your talents. Be the best you can be', and this served us well during the ten years of my headship.

One of my research participants explained that having led a detailed consultation exercise on the school's key priorities in his first term as a head, he then moved on to a full discussion of the core behaviours which demonstrated that these priorities were lived in the day-to-day operation of the school: the relationships, systems, protocols and policies which underpinned their educational beliefs. The head needs to work closely with the governing body on this and to secure the support of the different groups within the school community who are responsible for making this happen. But, in my experience, only the head can drive the process.

So the head needs to have a grasp of the big picture. While the deputy may be more involved in the day-to-day management and 'doing things right', the head's focus may be more strategic, taking a wider view and leading, 'doing the right things'. The head may also find that a fair amount of time is spent on PR, being the face of the school – a spokesperson and a figurehead. For me, a good deal of time was spent meeting prospective pupils and their parents and helping them to understand why our school might be the right place for their child to thrive. I had a clear sense that in some ways the head *is* the school. I remember in subsequent years a parent saying, 'We chose this school because we chose you – we bought into what you seemed to stand for.' This is a weighty responsibility: in some ways humbling, in some ways thrilling.

However, as head, especially in a new school, I realised I knew very little initially about the detail of how the school worked, something that as an established deputy in my previous school I had been secure and confident about. Of course it isn't *necessary* for the head to know the detail, and in my view nothing good can come from micromanaging. But heads must have the overview: they certainly need to know enough to gauge whether operations in different areas are going smoothly and where there is need for attention and adjustment. The head's job, arguably (in conjunction with the senior team), is to ensure that the right people are in the right jobs. This includes the senior leaders themselves, in addition to middle leaders, teachers and support staff. Offering the right balance of support and challenge at all levels should ensure that aspirations are high and standards are set and met, but the head has to be sufficiently relaxed not to worry that every detail of the school's operation is not tightly within their personal control.

Controlling everything would not be manageable and sustainable for a busy head, but neither would it be desirable. Heads are not the repository of all the best ideas. As York head teacher John Tomsett (2015: 98) says: 'It's not your idea, it's the best idea – and that might be hiding anywhere in your school.' Heads do need to win hearts and minds, to earn respect (which will not automatically come with the title) and to give and gain trust. The best leaders assume the staff they inherit are trustworthy, unless or until they have evidence to the contrary, at which point they have to take responsibility and act. But assuming that those you lead are not trustworthy, until you have evidence to the contrary, in my experience never ends well.

Although heads may have been privy to the judgements of their predecessors with respect to the competence of the staff they inherit, I would suggest an incoming head needs to give staff the opportunity to prove themselves and exercise their own judgement, rather than relying purely on the word of the outgoing head. Recognise and build on strengths, find out what people are good at, hunt down the bright spots and make the most of them, adopting an appreciative enquiry approach. But this does not mean turning a blind eye to practice which is not good enough.

Heads may well find that they are out of school more than they ever were as deputies, so they need to make decisions about what is the best use of their time – for their own development, for the good of the school, and also with respect to wider collaboration and making a contribution to the educational landscape beyond their school. As Andy Buck (2014) attests, successful schools look outward rather than battening down the hatches and only ever looking inward. However, there is a balance to be struck, and in the early months new heads, especially in a school they are still getting to know, have to ensure they are devoting sufficient time to building this knowledge – the broad brush strokes, if not the fine detail.

So, an understanding of some of the differences between the nature of the deputy's role and that of the head can help incoming heads to negotiate the process of transition. Raising your awareness, ensuring you are sufficiently reflective and that you critically examine any prior assumptions and preconceptions that might be misleading or unhelpful is certainly advisable. What else can you do to ensure that you make this transition successfully?

- Be informed. Use what you learnt during your time as a deputy about the critical differences between the head's role and the deputy's and how that affects the way the responsibilities are enacted. Take any opportunity to visit other heads and identify different ways in which individuals fulfil the role. This will help you in the early stages of stepping up to headship.

- Be alert. In discussion with your PA and senior team, find out as much as you can about how your predecessor organised their diary and managed their time. You will not necessarily fulfil the role in the same way as the previous head, but it is useful to be aware of the norms of practice you are inheriting and how the role differs from your deputy role. If your PA is able to tell you, 'In the past we have usually …' this gives you a useful starting point for how you might decide to behave and what you prioritise.

- Be proactive. Actively seek out other sources of information to help widen your perspective on the differences between the two roles. Do you have contacts (perhaps former colleagues) who are slightly further along the path than you are – one or two years into their headships – whom you can ask about where they found the deputy/head roles different and how they managed this? What challenges did they experience, what strategies did they use and what lessons did they learn that they are prepared to share with you?

- Be self-aware. Examine your own response to situations and be aware of falling into the trap of responding as a deputy might. Be prepared to let go (even if in some ways you feel as if you could have done the deputy's task better or more quickly!) and build mutual trust. Guard against any temptation to micromanage. Keep an eye on the bigger picture.

As one head says when reflecting on the first 100 days in the role:

One of the biggest differences I have found between being a Head and a deputy is emotion. For me, being a deputy meant working hard, learning as much as I could, doing a good job, pleasing my boss. But being a Head is much more emotional. For me, it means loving my school. (Dixon, 2007: 18)

Continuing to build the bridge as you walk on it

One of my research participants observed, as she reached the end of the lead-in period before officially stepping into the role:

> In a sense one sells oneself as a potential head as a kind of Meccano, a dot to dot ... This is what I will be when I am a head. But you don't actually know you can do it until you're doing it.

This idea of learning how to be a head from being a head was something to which all six of my research participants alluded – both in the time prior to appointment and when I met them a term into the role. One of them talked of the importance to her of 'being a head, not just doing the job', an interesting distinction which reinforces the sense of personal identity, self-belief and confidence. Others remarked that you only begin to see yourself as the head when you are confident that others within the school community see you in this way. Internal promotions can pose a particular challenge here, as those you lead begin to see you differently. You have taken a big step when you move into the head's office, and this may require a degree of re-education and a shift in perspective for both them and you.

So what did the reality of leading the school mean for my participants, and what unexpected challenges were they called upon to navigate? Three of my participants faced inspection at an early stage in their tenure. Although this was stressful in some respects, it did give a useful benchmark of where the school was, which could give added impetus to the sense of direction and where it was going under its new leadership. Although I would suggest that it is never advisable for heads and senior leaders to use inspection as a stick to beat people with ('We have to do this because inspection will demand that ...'), nevertheless, the recommendations which emerge from inspection can help to focus the mind and perhaps strengthen the arguments for making some of the changes that these incoming heads considered to be right for the school.

Leading the school through an inspection encouraged my participants to consider how different the head's role is from the deputy's at this time. Often deputies are key to the smooth running of the practicalities of the inspection process. The head's role will be broader, with less involvement in the nitty-gritty of the arrangements, but importantly they will model positivity, receptivity and openness to feedback and confidence that the process should enable the school to demonstrate clearly and achieve recognition for the things it does well (the bright spots), in addition to considering those areas where there is scope for development. So the head was called upon to rally the troops through the inspection process while their deputies managed the detail.

Three participants dealt with difficult bereavements in their first weeks, something which could not have been anticipated or prepared for, and arguably this kind of challenge is one of the most difficult things a school community has to face. One new head was confronted with the unexpected death of her head girl's father. Another coped with the repercussions of the sudden death of a 19-year-old former pupil in the summer holiday immediately preceding the head's arrival – one of three brothers who had attended the school and whose parents were based abroad, so the school became the focus of the memorial service.

The third situation was the most difficult of all. My participant had negotiated with her predecessor, who was moving to a second headship, that when the A level results were released each would remain in their current school. My participant had taught a Year 13 class as a deputy and was keen to see and congratulate members of a year group she knew well before she left that school. Her predecessor in the school to which she was moving was keen to do the same. However, for GCSE results, each would move to her new school. The cohort collecting their results, although not known to these incoming heads, constituted the members of their first lower sixth. Being with them on GCSE results day offered a valuable opportunity to begin to build relationships with this year group.

The week before GCSE results were released, my participant was on holiday when she received a telephone call from the school to which she was moving as head. One of the pupils in Year 11 had been involved in a tragic accident and had subsequently died. This 16-year-old would have been coming to the school to collect GCSE results, alongside the rest of the year group, on the incoming head's first official day in post.

Dealing with such incredibly difficult issues is taxing for all those within the school, and it requires sensitivity, calmness and good judgement. These new heads did not have established relationships with the students involved, their families or the staff and pupils affected by the tragedy. They had to rely heavily on the knowledge and advice of their senior teams and governors as to how the school needed to respond. In the case of two sudden pupil deaths, this meant that the start of the term was significantly more sombre and muted than it otherwise might have been. Although these new heads would have already given thought to what they intended to say in their first full-school assembly and their initial whole-staff meeting, the unexpected tragic events meant that they had to rethink and revisit the tone and content of both.

Unanticipated events which challenge new heads in the early days offer an opportunity for them to show their strength and to prove to others, and to themselves, that they are capable of stepping up to the challenge and leading their schools even in the most difficult times. They will need to rely on other members of their school community, and relationships may be strengthened as a result. The new head of the school which mourned the death of the Year 11 pupil was aware that the situation brought the senior team closer together. The head whose school was organising the memorial service for the 19-year-old former pupil recognised that this gave him the opportunity to interact with a large number of former pupils and their families at an early stage in his tenure. However, such challenges require professionalism and an emotional resilience which will clearly make significant demands on all those affected.

Other participants dealt with unforeseen challenges of a different order, which nevertheless caused them to question their assumptions and preconceptions. One incoming head opened up his laptop in his new school to discover that there was little wireless connectivity across the campus, reflecting the fact that the school was at a very early stage in its use of educational technology. This was completely different from the school where he had been a deputy and the school in which he had taught prior to that, and it took him by surprise. The same head also discovered an imbalance in staffing across the school, with a large number of part-time teachers which he felt skewed the timetable and impacted negatively on the staff's capacity to contribute to the school's extra-curricular provision. This was not something he had picked up during the lead-in period, and it caused him concern.

There were also a number of unexpected challenges which arose from contrasting role expectations – both in the way the new school community expected the head's role to be enacted and also where the head had certain expectations of the staff they inherited which did not align with their predecessor's practice. As one new head said, 'I think I probably didn't quite realise how sensitive staff are to change. I didn't envisage how nerve-wracking the change of head is for just a normal member of staff. And I think that's quite hard to know until you're in it.' Another observed, 'Because you're new, you're going to be different. You don't come in with the intention of changing things. But just by your very nature you're going to be conceived as something very different.'

One interesting experience encountered by the latter new head involved preparations for the annual Harvest Festival in the school into which she had moved:

> There was one example where people's perceptions are so important. While I was perceiving myself as being very open and wanting to be involved, my deputy perceived the situation as threatening and intimidating.
>
> It was in preparation for the Harvest Festival. There was a practice scheduled on the timetable. I'd actually made sure I could go along. I literally sat at the back and was enjoying it, just being part of it. But afterwards it came out when I next saw the deputy she'd actually

felt threatened and didn't see it as support. She didn't know whether she was still in charge and was unsure what to do and what to say. She didn't know whether I was going to say everything. It was probably the way that it had been handled by the previous head – if she was there, she was the person in charge, whereas I was deliberately, even in my body language, stepping back.

When we discussed what she felt she had learnt from this incident my participant said, 'My idea of valuing people, wanting to be open, some are actually perceiving as threatening.' The key issue here is what the new head decides to do when they realise that their actions have been misunderstood or misinterpreted: they recognise they need to communicate their intentions and expectations more clearly. This new head had a full and frank discussion with her deputy after the Harvest Festival incident, and said that this was how she would show her interest in, and support of, events in the school – being visible but not interfering. She tried to reassure her deputy that, 'In future you will know that it's not me judging you.'

However, although these new heads sometimes recalibrated their actions in the light of such information about others' perceptions, and perhaps others' anxiety, they did not necessarily dramatically change the way they enacted the head's role. They did not automatically seek to align their way of leading with the way their predecessor had led the school – the way the school community might be used to and feel comfortable with. They were working to inhabit the role and not simply to inherit it.

In some cases they were explicit about this when they talked to the staff. For example, one said at her first staff meeting, 'The last head was excellent. She did an excellent handover to me, but I'm not her. I'm never going to be her. I'm not going to try to be her. All I can say to you is that I am myself, and I will do my very best.'

If a new head takes over from a relatively autocratic, perhaps controlling, head, and their strong conviction is that they should be more consultative and democratic, it is easy to make the assumption that the staff will welcome this. However, if the staff are unaccustomed to being asked what they think, incoming leaders can find this takes some adapting to before they feel sufficiently confident to take full advantage of the opportunity offered to them. Incoming heads need to tune in to the context, recognise expectations, and sometimes insecurities, and work to build confidence and trust. Sometimes the school community needs educating about different ways of leading. Sometimes the incoming head needs educating about what is possible, and what is advisable, in the early stages of their headship. As one of my participants commented, 'This is maybe part of what leadership is, being able to adapt.'

So, in the early months in post, you inherit a great deal – a governing body, a senior team, a PA – but also a legacy of norms and expectations, a sense of 'how things are done here' where the head's leadership is concerned. My firm advice is that you do not have to be constrained by this, although you ignore it at your peril. You have to be sensitive to the context and to the views of the community you join. This is not just about your journey. Transition involves a process of transformation for both the new school leader and the led.

Sometimes you have to act, evaluate, recalibrate and adjust, a process head teacher Tom Sherrington (2015) refers to as 'Ready, fire, aim'. It may be impossible to predict with complete accuracy how initiatives will be received and how the changes you are implementing will develop. In the early months of a new headship you will need to listen attentively, think carefully, be receptive to all you can learn, and adjust your understanding and your actions accordingly. However, this does not mean that you slip into role-taking and inheriting. You will no doubt determine to make this job your own, to make your mark on the role and the school, and this will involve negotiating the tensions between role-taking and role-making, between inheriting and inhabiting, in your early months in post and in the months and years which follow.

Questions for reflection

■ Can you identify any connections, or emerging tensions, between the leader you hope to be, the leader this particular school currently requires you to be and the leader the school will allow you to be at this stage of your tenure?

■ What strategies can you use for building positive relationships with the different groups within the school community? Are different strategies required for pupils, staff, senior leaders, parents, prospective parents and governors?

■ If you are internally promoted, are you clear about how your relationship with these groups may change, and how you will manage this?

■ What are the most significant bright spots on which you hope to build?

■ In terms of areas for development, what do you consider should take priority in your first weeks, in your first term and in your first year?

■ If you have decided to teach, can you clearly explain your rationale for doing so? Will you share your reasoning with pupils, staff, parents and governors? And if you decide not to teach, do you also have a rationale?

■ Can you identify any early shocks and surprises with respect to the differences between the role of the deputy and the role of the head? What lessons have you learnt as a result, and how has this helped you to grow into your new role?

■ Have you managed any critical incidents and, if so, can you see any way in which the experience has given you the opportunity to prove yourself?

Chapter 5

Established headship and beyond

Moving beyond being the 'new head'

I was recently involved in conducting some research into the challenges heads currently face and how they can be better supported, for example, by governors. This was broader than my doctoral research focus in that it looked at established heads, rather than just newly appointed heads, and it wasn't specifically to do with making the transition to first headship. One head I interviewed looked back at his time as a school leader and commented, rather ruefully:

> I experienced a new heads' induction programme before I took up the post, and had a follow-up day a few months into my headship. I also had a mentor in my first year.
>
> The problem is, you don't stop being a new head at the end of your first year.

So when do you stop feeling like a 'new head' and become an established school leader?

With respect to this specific research project, we considered heads in their first three years of leadership to be 'new heads', and those in year four onwards to be 'experienced heads', but, of course, this is an arbitrary distinction. New heads do experience a 'honeymoon period', where those they lead may wish to create a favourable impression on the incoming school leader and so be on their best behaviour. The governors who have appointed you may seem particularly biddable and agreeable, and your requests may be met, at least initially, with a favourable, positive response. Enjoy this time; it seems to me that if you don't enjoy the honeymoon, it doesn't augur well for the marriage. But recognise that it will not last forever. (And there is no blueprint as to how long it will last. Ask experienced heads you know how long they considered the honeymoon period to be and I suspect that there will be a range of responses!)

In their research into the different stages of headship, based on a longitudinal study of a large group of head teachers from the 1980s onwards, Earley and Weindling (2004) conclude that heads go through seven different phases from the lead-in period through to being an established head. Their suggestion as to the focus of these stages is as follows:

Stage 0: Preparation prior to headship

Stage 1: Entry and encounter (first months)

Stage 2: Taking hold (three to twelve months)

Stage 3: Reshaping (second year)

Stage 4: Refinement (years three to four)

Stage 5: Consolidation (years five to seven)

Stage 6: Plateau (year eight and onwards)

I have kept in close contact with a group of new heads who all started, as I did, in 2000. We met twice a year throughout my ten years of headship (and, in fact, continue to meet periodically and support each other today, sixteen years after we first met as heads-elect). I remember meeting for lunch in London in 2005 and one of the group saying, 'I didn't think it would be this hard in year five ...'

In my experience, you have never 'cracked it' and headship never becomes mundane, routine and easy. The challenges may change, and your confidence and experience inevitably grow, but you never feel that your learning is complete and you have the full set of head teacher skills mastered and secure. I remember having days as a head when I thought, 'I'm actually doing OK at this job,' followed by days when I felt, 'Who am I kidding? I'm barely getting away with it and one day someone will find me out ...' Imposter syndrome may never be far away.

My view is that this reflects the complex nature of your responsibilities, the multifaceted role you fill and the large number of people and situations you encounter in the process. I was shadowed a number of times during my years of headship: once by the executive director of the heads' association of which I was a member, once by my new chair of governors and on several occasions by aspiring heads who wanted to learn more about the role. I remember one of these observers remarking at the end of the day:

> Everybody wants a piece of you. And somehow at the end of each day you have to find a way to put yourself back together again.

How can you sustain this over the course of your headship, ensuring that you pace yourself successfully and that you achieve a sustainable balance in your life so that you have the energy to do what needs to be done without too great a personal cost? How can you protect yourself so that the job does not subsume you, and how can you take care to protect your personal well-being and relationships so that you don't neglect them in the face of potentially overwhelming professional relationships and responsibilities?

Making the most of the joy of headship

One of the pieces of advice I received when I was a deputy considering headship came from a head a few years into the role who shared this:

> You will have some tough days where you will need to be reminded about the good bits. Keep a 'Positive Book'. Put into it anything that gives you a warm glow – a letter of thanks, a note of appreciation, anything that is positive about the school or your leadership of it. There may be days where you need to leaf through it. It will help to remind you that there is a brighter side to headship.

I took this advice and started what I called my 'Happy File' – a lever arch collection of those letters, notes, cards and positive messages, some about the school and some about my contribution to it. By the time I left after ten years this ran to several volumes. I still treasure the Happy Files and know they are something to which I will return periodically for the rest of my life.

And perhaps I was fortunate, but it seems to me that the positive experiences and the good days significantly outnumbered the negative. There were challenges and some difficult issues to navigate; I was tested and I know that I made mistakes and sometimes lacked courage. But I learnt and I believe I grew in the role. I was a more resilient head in year ten than I had been in year one – I was always sensitive, and continue to believe that sensitivity is a significant strength, but I was aware that my capacity to 'get over it' and bounce back quickly improved as the years passed. I certainly found the role fulfilling and rewarding. I definitely found joy in headship.

I was conscious that as a head I had greater autonomy than I had ever had before, and relished the opportunity to make decisions (for example, with respect to how I used my time) rather than to seek approval or permission from others. It helped that I found my governing body supportive and always felt that they had confidence in me. I found governing body meetings energising, though they could be appropriately challenging: sometimes I faced tough questions which required thoughtful and robust answers. But I always felt the governors were on my side – and this continued to be the case even though over the course of my headship some governors left us and others joined us, with the result that the governing body I worked with in the last days of my headship was a completely different group from the one which had appointed me eleven years earlier.

I enjoyed teaching, and the opportunity that it gave me to build relationships with individual pupils (see Chapter 4 for the detail of how I structured this) and, through them, with their parents. Because I had taught them and knew them (and they knew me), pupils often introduced me to their parents at parents' evenings and other school events. I also remember a girl in Year 11 coming to my office door one day to tell me how thrilled she was to have organised her work experience at *Vogue* magazine. After she had left, I reflected that she probably wouldn't have felt sufficiently confident to do that had I not taught her several years earlier.

I described in the previous chapter how I took the decision in the early weeks and months (actually beginning during the lead-in period) to support as many different extra-curricular events as I could. Having begun my headship in this way it then simply became what I always did. I joined the choir and sang alongside the staff and girls. I attended as many sports fixtures as I could fit in – even if this meant I could only call in for a short time, to cheer and encourage before I shot off to another commitment. As an English specialist interested in drama I especially enjoyed accompanying theatre trips and, of course, attending rehearsals and productions in school. I loved visiting the different clubs and societies and seeing what staff and students were experiencing and achieving. I had moved to a school which had a Combined Cadet Force, a new experience for me, and it was thrilling to go sailing, flying and joining fieldcraft activities with groups of cadets – and I joined Duke of Edinburgh's Award scheme walks too.

Residential trips of all kinds, at home and abroad, were hugely enjoyable and enabled me to build relationships with pupils, staff and parents further. I went on a Year 6 adventure holiday to France, a history department trip to the First World War battlefields, a German exchange visit to Celle, a swimming tour to Malta, a drama trip to Greece. I relished the company of students and staff, and know they appreciated my interest. I went to watch, listen and learn – I was not in charge, and made very clear to the party organisers that I was there in the capacity of an accompanying member of staff, not the head, and in that context they had the authority. In the same way, I told the head of English that with respect to my English lessons I was a member of her department and would do whatever she wanted me to do.

So the enjoyment, and the feeling of pride which came from all these experiences as I watched members of the school contributing, achieving, working and playing together, was all bound up, for me, with the joy of headship. Watching these students grow and develop over time, build their confidence and maturity with the support and encouragement of the staff – and an appropriate degree of healthy challenge – was hugely satisfying and pleasurable. Watching the staff themselves grow, sometimes moving on to fresh challenges within or beyond the school, and having the opportunity to support the development of their teaching and leadership skills, was energising.

I was acutely aware of the importance of trying to model leadership positively. I hoped to encourage future generations of leaders at all levels to see the rewards and the benefits of having a leadership role, rather than simply to be mindful of the pressures, stress and responsibility. It seemed to me that if members of the school community (including the pupils) did not see the positive elements of leadership, this would be a betrayal of those who had the potential to lead, in whatever capacity and whatever organisation, in the years to come.

The pupils who were 7 years old when I started at the school were in the sixth form by the time I left, ready to embark on the next stage of the adventure. It is interesting to reflect on how little you may feel you have changed as you move from the age of 40 to 50, compared with the transition those ten years represent when you move from being 7 to 17. I loved watching the growth and development of young people over time, and knowing that the school I led had made a positive contribution to this, offering opportunities and providing guidance and support during difficult periods.

In my first year as a head I made the decision to read each pupil's full report, including all the individual subject comments, to sign it by hand and to add comments of my own where I thought they were appropriate. As time passed and I taught more and more pupils, and got to know them as individuals, I moved to writing a comment on every report. This was very time consuming but, in fact, interesting and satisfying, because it underlined for me how these learners were changing and developing over time. It gave me a very good insight into the staff, too – their teaching and pastoral styles, their priorities, their relationships. I was able to form a view of how well they knew these young people and how successfully they nurtured them, in addition to whether they had appropriately high aspirations which they worked hard to help the learners meet.

As the years passed I had, of course, appointed an increasing number of these staff and that, too, was rewarding: seeing adults fulfil their potential over time also brings a sense of achievement and satisfaction, as does helping those who need your support to address issues and emerge stronger on the other side. Over the ten years I served as head I was able to appoint five new members of the senior leadership team – and was proud of the calibre of the team I left as a legacy for my successor.

My role as head enabled me to build relationships with families, too, sometimes supporting them through difficult times. Sharing concern for and commitment to the young people at the centre of our relationship was a way of cementing the bond between home and school. I also enjoyed meeting significant numbers of former students and staff whose links to the school, and whose support of it, remained strong. And in the capacity of head of the school, I established connections with members of the wider community, often representing the school beyond its gates and feeling proud and privileged to do so.

Returning to my six research participants and considering their experiences of the early months of headship, I could see ways in which they, too, were relishing the opportunities the role was already bringing and which they could see it would continue to offer in the years ahead:

> I love the fact that I can now begin to carve the vision myself.

> Maybe 15% of my first term has been a headache. But the other 85% has been frenetic fun!

> When I leave the house each morning I feel energised. I feel positive, and I look forward to the challenge.

And:

> My advice for any new head starting, going in – people will look to you to lead. Regardless of who you've taken over from, it's a new person, and they want to follow you instinctively. They want to be led. And it's a joy to lead them.

This final quotation reinforces the fact that a change of head can be energising. An incoming head can be a powerful catalyst for change. Staff expect things to be different, and if the new head is too respectful of existing ways of doing things, or too cautious about moving forward, the impetus could be lost. Being respectful of the context of your new school and finding the right pace and an appropriate balance is the key.

Balance and sustainability

Headship was my seventh job in my sixth school. The longest I had stayed in any school prior to this was five years and a term, and that was my first school where I was internally promoted. When I was interviewed for the headship, one of the questions I was asked was, 'How long do you think you will remain as head in this school?' This wasn't a question I had anticipated, so it wasn't a question for which I was mentally prepared. I found myself saying, 'Ten years,' with some conviction.

It may have been because my predecessor had been in the school for ten years, or because it took eleven years for a pupil to progress from Year 3 to Year 13. Or it may just have been because ten years sounded like a good, solid block of time to serve a school as head, to establish yourself, introduce initiatives and see them properly embedded. For whatever reason I chose ten years, it turned out, for me, to have been the right answer.

I don't believe that, as a head, it is possible to do a worthwhile job unless you are prepared to invest at least five years in the role. And I think heads should be wary of staying in one school for too long, when it may be that they have lost the freshness of perception and the clarity of vision with respect to how the school needs to be evolving and developing, or the energy to make it happen. Ten years felt right for me. I had a sense that, although I still enjoyed the role and loved the school, it might be ready for a different kind of head, with a different temperament and skill set, in 2010, compared with the head it had appointed back in 1999.

I was also mindful that the role, although potentially joyful, is taxing and can be draining, and it requires reserves of energy that might be starting to become depleted ten years in. Heads do need to pace themselves. It is possible to burn out and to become less, rather than more, effective as a result. In fact, it has been suggested that heads are at their most effective between years three and seven (Mortimore, 1998), and after that the law of diminishing returns begins to take effect. Brighouse and Woods (2013: 56) also attest: 'We haven't met too many heads whose second ten years were better than their first.'

I do believe in the importance of heads working to achieve a sustainable balance in their lives, and modelling this positively to the rest of the school community. In addition to trying to get the balance right for themselves, leaders at all levels have a responsibility for monitoring and supporting those they lead to do the same. And this is hard.

There is no single, simple way to do this. We all have to make decisions about how hard we are prepared to work, how many hours we are willing to invest in our professional commitments, and when we need to stop and rest. The work – as a teacher and as a leader in a school – is never completed. Generally we work as hard as we demand of ourselves, rather than just being driven by those who lead and manage us or by external forces (Ofsted and the Independent Schools Inspectorate, the Department for Education and the government). There are certainly external pressures and requirements, but I believe we have more agency than we sometimes give ourselves credit for. Arguably, heads have more agency than others within schools, and they can make choices about what they are and are not prepared to do, and what they will demand of others.

This is a sensitive and controversial area, and not all will agree with me, but I feel strongly that we have to beware of seeing ourselves as victims where workload and work/ life balance are concerned, and consider where we can take responsibility for finding a personal/professional balance which is reasonable and workable. Can we learn from positive role models around us who seem to be getting the balance right? Remember that if it is not possible to do a conscientious and committed job and still have a life, there is something wrong with the job, not with you.

I was dedicated as a teacher, a middle leader, a senior leader and a head. I certainly worked hard in each role and in each school. I worked harder as a head than I had ever done prior to that point – both in terms of the hours I put in and with respect to the difficulty of some of the issues I had to tackle and the judgement calls I had to make. I still found it the most enjoyable and rewarding of all the jobs I had across my thirty-year career.

I felt strongly, however, that I did not want to be defined by my professional persona, and that when you took the 'head teacher' out of me, there would still be a person left behind. If all our self-worth derives from our professional identity, this can be quite dangerous. People lose their jobs. This is a job, not your entire life, and not the sum total of who you are.

A former colleague of mine, with a well-established, successful career, visited the doctor for a routine check-up, and the doctor asked her to tell him what were the three most important things in her life. She chose her family and friends as the most important, her health and well-being as the next, and her career as the third. He then asked her how much of her time she allocated to those three things. This made her thoughtful. She had to admit that probably she devoted around 80% of her time to her career, leaving the two most important elements of her life to share the remaining 20% between them. This fuelled her conviction to take early retirement in due course. She had loved her job and had been committed to it, but she knew it was only a part of who she was, and she wanted time to give to those other important aspects which she felt made her life worth living.

While you are a head, you need to think about how to look after your health and well-being, and do the best job you can, by ensuring you are not exhausted or so stressed that you lose the capacity to think clearly and act appropriately. You need to build your self-awareness and know yourself well enough to gauge when you should keep working and when you need to stop, rest and refresh, because you will do a better job if you stop now and pick it up later. You need thinking time – and time for reflection can be difficult to generate when you are busy reacting to the demands and challenges which come your way.

So how can it be done? Consider the following strategies and which might work best for you in your context:

- Supportive networks, role models, mentors and coaches will continue to be important in your professional life. Although you hope to have a positive

relationship with your governors and your senior
team, there are many benefits to being able to talk
through issues and strategies with someone who
is to some degree detached and dispassionate (and
not a subordinate or an employer). Sometimes you
do not need anyone to advise you – you just need
the opportunity to use someone who cares and
understands as a sounding board to help you think
through clearly and articulate what steps you should
take. Consider engaging a personal coach if you
cannot identify anyone who quite fits the bill. Your
governing body should be committed to supporting
you by investing in this and ensuring you continue
to develop personally and professionally. Support
is not only required by heads who are experiencing
difficulties. Be prepared to have that full and frank
conversation with your governing body if you do
not feel they are getting the balance of support and
challenge right.

- A regular process of professional review should help
  you to recognise your strengths and achievements and
  to ensure these are formally recorded and properly
  valued. Any appraisal process should not simply focus
  on externally set targets and accountability. This is not
  just a mechanism for your governors/employers to
  check your competence. It should also be supportive
  and challenging in a positive and productive way,
  helping you, for example, to identify and feel good
  about the bright spots as well as to clarify your
  thinking about areas of focus for the twelve months
  ahead.

- Contributing to the world of education beyond your individual school can also help you to keep a sense of perspective and a clear view of the big picture. Supporting other educators can encourage you to look at the challenges you face through a broader lens.

- Showing gratitude is another way of generating positive feelings. When we communicate our appreciation of the contribution of those around us, there is a distinct two-way benefit. Never underestimate the power of the brief handwritten note.

- Having interests beyond education can also be refreshing, especially something which requires you to concentrate and focus in such a way that you are not able to dwell on school-related issues. Music or physical exercise, for example, can provide a very useful release and relief from the professional pressures you face each day.

- Spending a good block of time with friends and family outside the world of education and replenishing your positive energies can give you a boost to go back to work with renewed impetus and motivation. Weekends and holidays are important here; you may find you need to use part of each weekend and part of your holiday time to catch up and to plan ahead, but I strongly believe that you also need to spend part of each weekend and a substantial chunk of each holiday resting and refreshing and trying not to think about school. This is more difficult than it sounds, I know, but if you are constantly dwelling on school-related issues you may find that you are not unwinding effectively, and when term starts you already feel jaded rather than refreshed and re-energised.

- With respect to the last point, decide how accessible you wish to be to school personnel and concerns. Can you physically detach from the electronic devices that connect you to your professional persona so that you are not constantly at the beck and call of the school community, including parents? I would suggest that someone in the school (your PA, perhaps, or your chair of governors or senior team) should always know how to contact you in the event of an emergency, but constantly checking emails, for example, does not allow you the space you need to take a breath and clear your head. If you use Twitter to connect with professional networks (a strategy I strongly recommend), be disciplined about when you are going to check it. If you use Twitter to connect with family and friends as well, keep two separate accounts.

We need to be self-disciplined. It is easy to defend the 24/7 (and 365 days a year) preoccupation with school by telling yourself that you enjoy it, that you want to know what is going on, and that you are responsible and so have to be easily contactable and always accessible. Sometimes this can be addictive and takes considerable self-control to break away from. Guilt can be a most unproductive emotion. Again, know yourself. Driving yourself harder and harder and never taking a proper break will not make you a better head. It might make you a considerably less effective one. Carving out time for yourself, your friends and family, your interests, and your own health and well-being is not selfish or irresponsible. It is, in my view, essential.

And if you model this to the school community, there is the greater likelihood that others, too, will work to achieve a sustainable, sensible balance in their lives and, as a result, achieve greater professional effectiveness. 'I will work harder' should never be the automatic response to each new challenge. It did not turn out well for the cart-horse Boxer in Orwell's *Animal Farm*, and I suggest it will not work for you and for those you lead either.

Next steps?

So what comes after headship?

I was 41 when I was appointed to my headship and 42 when I officially stepped into the role. I had begun teaching straight after my degree and PGCE at 22, so it had taken me twenty years to reach headship. At the time, in 2000, I felt like quite a young head; at gatherings of head teachers I often seemed to be one of the youngest.

These days, heads may reach that point considerably earlier. They may be 'fast-tracked' along the way. They may be career changers who come into teaching having had significant leadership experience in other fields and so progress through the levels of middle and senior leadership quickly. At the other end of their career, accessing their teachers' pension at the age of 60, as I am able to do, is no longer possible for newer entrants to the profession. The expected retirement age may continue to recede over the horizon.

After ten years of headship, at the age of 52, I decided to do something different with the last professionally useful stretch of my life. Much as I enjoyed headship, and still enthuse about it, I have never had any regrets about making that decision. My life is rich and rewarding and I fully appreciate having more time, and more choices, than I felt I had when working full-time. I explained earlier that I find professional transitions fascinating: what motivates a classroom teacher to want to move to a middle leadership role? Why do some middle leaders aspire to become senior leaders with whole-school responsibility? Why do some senior leaders 'make the leap' to headship? And what about the next transition – what comes after that?

It seems to me that children of the 1950s and 1960s, like me, made career choices which were lifelong. I became a teacher in 1980 and my career decision was made. Other contemporaries became lawyers, medics and so on. In the latter stages of my time as a teacher I recognised that the pupils we taught were far more likely to have wide-ranging and varied professional lives; they might well teach but only for a time. They might work abroad for a stretch, run their own business, try different professional arenas. It meant that those of us who were helping to prepare them for the professional challenges ahead had to consider how these learners could be supported to develop a variety of skills, in addition to adaptability, resilience, determination and motivation.

So what about the head teachers of tomorrow and the options that will be open to them beyond their first headship? What might your future path look like, and what course would suit you in your personal context?

One of the considerations will be financial, of course. Do you need to continue to earn a salary, or to generate sufficient income in a self-employed capacity, to provide for yourself and your dependants? If money is not an issue, there is a wide range of voluntary activities which might bring you satisfaction and a sense of purpose, and for which the multiple skills you have developed as a teacher and school leader fit you well. If you are still keen to contribute to the world of education – for example, by joining a governing body (or more than one) – the expertise and insights you have to offer could be invaluable, and you have the opportunity to make a positive contribution which you may find rewarding.

You might decide, as I did, to spend some time on further academic qualifications. My professional doctorate stretched me, made me think deeply and consolidated my learning, both about the process of research and the research subject – in my case, the transition to headship. This may also lead to opportunities to be involved in other research projects which may generate income.

If, however, you wish to, or need to, keep earning a substantial amount, then consider the following:

- Moving to a subsequent headship, or more than one in due course, may well be the 'norm' for those who have experienced a first headship and are ready for a fresh challenge. You might wish to consider a school or another educational establishment in a different sector, phase or country. The key thing here will be ensuring you successfully tune in to the context of your new school (using the lead-in period, again, as productively as possible), and do not assume that you know how to do the job. The new context may require you to enact the role, at least initially, in quite a different way, while still being true to who you are and what you stand for.

- Moving to lead a group of schools – for example, in the capacity of an executive principal – will allow you to draw on all you have learnt as the head of a single school, but will also require a different focus and an extension of the skills you have developed up to this point. Successful prior leadership of an individual school should give you credibility and a valuable understanding of the perspective and priorities of the individual school leaders across the group you join.

- Moving into another role in an educational organisation with a wider brief and a different set of challenges might also appeal. Again, the fact that you have been a head should strengthen your application and allow for successful transfer into a new, but in some ways related, professional identity.

- Moving into a consultancy role, either as an associate working with other organisations or on a self-employed basis, perhaps setting yourself up as a small/medium business enterprise, might appeal to you, as it did to me. I have enjoyed working with governors on heads' and senior leaders' appointments; conducting heads' and senior leaders' appraisals/professional reviews; staff training, usually leadership related, within schools and for different organisations; coaching and mentoring. Such consultancy work may give you the opportunity to share your expertise and focus on those elements of education and of school leadership in which you are most interested. You will need to build contacts and promote your consultancy services. I have found online networking, such as LinkedIn and Twitter, a very good way of forging connections which have been professionally useful. I have also found that writing for educational publications, both print and online, links successfully to consultancy work, enabling you to build a professional profile which can lead to a range of opportunities. Embarking on this book project has been part of that process, and neatly connects, for me, my professional experience, my research, my consultancy work and my educational commentary activity.

There will be, of course, a range of paid opportunities beyond the world of education, too, depending on your interests, skills and passions. Several former heads I know have joined non-executive boards and have developed their interests and expertise in a variety of professional areas. There is a wealth of opportunity out there. As you did when you embarked on headship applications, it is all about finding (and then clearly demonstrating) the match between what is needed and what you have to offer.

For me, supporting aspiring and serving leaders at all levels has been an extremely positive and worthwhile experience. It allows me to integrate my own experience, my reading and research, my consultancy activity and my commitment to engaging with a broad network of educators through the world of Twitter and blogs. I consider myself fortunate that I am able to marry my interests and my passions with an opportunity to meet and work with a huge variety of inspiring leaders and future leaders. I am happily busy but still have time for myself and for my interests beyond education, for my family and friends, and for my health and well-being.

Questions for reflection

■ What steps are you taking to ensure that you sustain yourself throughout your headship, however long that may be? How can you avoid burn-out?

■ How long do you consider it might be appropriate for you to stay in your current role? Can you clearly articulate the reasons for your answer?

■ Consider your current personal/professional balance. Are you reasonably satisfied with it, or does it need recalibrating? If the latter, give serious thought to exactly how you can redress and improve it. Start with something small and make it work!

■ How well are you maintaining the supportive networks you have access to? Consider what you contribute to these networks, in addition to what you gain. Do your networks need more attention?

■ Does your appraisal/professional review process act as a positive reinforcement and clear record of what is going well, as well as helping you to clarify your thinking about future areas of focus? If not, draft notes to help you to prepare for a frank conversation with your chair of governors about this.

■ What do you contribute to the world of education beyond your school? If currently relatively little, is

> this something to build on (for mutual benefit) in the years ahead?
>
> ◼ If you are considering moving to a second headship at some stage, how do you think you could begin to prepare for this fresh challenge?
>
> ◼ If you envisage a different professional future beyond headship of a single school, consider the options described in this chapter. Make notes on the extent to which each alternative appeals to you and how well suited you believe you would be.

Headship is, in my view, a fascinating, challenging, rewarding and joyful occupation. It will tax you but it will also offer you the opportunity to grow and develop in the role, as you prove yourself to yourself and to those you lead. For my last words I return to my six research participants, deputies who moved to headship in 2013, and from whose journeys I learnt a good deal which supplemented my own experience and wider reading about leadership. I wish them all success and happiness, wherever the journey takes them.

> I think what I'm looking forward to most is being able to effect change and development about something which I'm passionate about, which is education. My particular passion is the development both of children and of adults.

> As a deputy you're behind the scenes organising everything, the person in the shadows, and maybe being there and then handing it over – but I'm actually going to be the person, that final person.

I'm keen to sell a vision of what I think is vital and which will set the tone for my headship ... This is what I stand for.

You've got that growing ball of anxiety ... because suddenly it's all becoming real and the expectation to deliver is there. But at the same time – yeah! I'm buzzing!

I can actually be the person who leads and supports, and it's going to be truly my school.

It takes a while to actually come to terms with it and believe it and I found that, over time, the more I've come into the school and got to know the people – met the children, met the staff, met the parents – the more I feel comfortable and thinking, yes, I actually can do this, because I have the experience, I have skills. No, I don't know everything now, but I've got support networks there.

There comes a point where you have read everything you could possibly read. You've done all the background you can, you've met the staff. There comes a point where you have to just get on with it, from day one, and you actually learn the job from the experience of doing the job.

You've got this huge anticipation. And then you're actually sitting in the chair. You're doing it! You've made the leap.

References and recommended reading

Bannister, N. (2013) The tyranny of stuff, *Headteacher Update* (10 January). Available at: http://www.headteacher-update.com/best-practice-article/the-tyranny-of-stuff/66690.

Barber, M., Whelan, F. and Clark, M. (2010) *Capturing the Leadership Premium: How the World's Top School Systems are Building Leadership Capacity for the Future.* New York: McKinsey and Company.

Berger, R. (2003) *An Ethic of Excellence: Building a Culture of Craftsmanship with Students.* Portsmouth, NH: Heinemann.

Brighouse, T. and Woods, D. (2013) *The A–Z of School Improvement: Principles and Practice.* London: Bloomsbury.

Buck, A. (2014) *What Makes a Great School: A Practical Formula for School Success* (Kindle edn). London: Leadership Matters.

Buck, A. (2016) *Leadership Matters: How Leaders At All Levels Can Create Great Schools.* Woodbridge: John Catt.

Bush, T. (2009) Leadership development and school improvement: contemporary issues in leadership development, *Educational Review* 61(4): 375–389.

Carman, D. (2013) *Heads Up: The Challenges Facing England's Leading Head Teachers.* London: Thistle.

Collins, J. (2001) *Good to Great.* London: Random House.

Despontin, B. (2007) The role of the head, in B. Despontin and N. Richardson (eds), *Heads: Expert Advice for Changing Times* (Leading Schools in the 21st Century series). Woodbridge: John Catt Educational, pp. 11–15.

Despontin, B. and Richardson, N. (eds) (2007) *Heads: Expert Advice for Changing Times* (Leading Schools in the 21st Century series). Woodbridge: John Catt Educational.

Dixon, G. (2007) The first hundred days, in B. Despontin and N. Richardson (eds), *Heads: Expert Advice for Changing Times* (Leading Schools in the 21st Century series). Woodbridge: John Catt Educational, pp. 17–27.

Earley, P. and Weindling, D. (2004) *Understanding School Leadership*. London: SAGE.

Gronn, P. (1999) *The Making of Educational Leaders*. London: Cassell.

Hargreaves, A. and Fink, D. (2006) *Sustainable Leadership*. San Francisco, CA: Jossey-Bass.

Harris, B. (2007) *Supporting the Emotional Work of School Leaders*. London: PCP.

Heath, C. and Heath, D. (2010) *Switch: How to Change Things When Change Is Hard*. London: Random House.

Jefferis, T. J. (2016) Leading the conversation: the use of Twitter by school leaders for professional development as their careers progress. EdD thesis, University of Birmingham. Available at: http://etheses.bham.ac.uk/6858/.

Leithwood, K., Day, C., Sammons, P., Harris, A. and Hopkins, D. (2006) *Seven Strong Claims about Successful School Leadership*. Nottingham: National College for School Leadership.

Matthews, L. and Crow, G. (2003) *Being and Becoming a Principal: Role Conceptions of Contemporary Principals and Assistant Principals*. Boston, MA: Pearson Education.

McGough, R. (1985) *Sky in the Pie*. London: Puffin.

Mortimore, P. (1998) *School Matters*. Berkeley, CA: University of California Press.

Myatt, M. (2016) *High Challenge, Low Threat: Finding the Balance*. Woodbridge: John Catt.

Pendleton, D. and Furnham, A. (2012) *Leadership: All You Need to Know*. Basingstoke: Palgrave Macmillan.

Quinn, R. (2004) *Building the Bridge As You Walk On It: A Guide for Leading Change*. San Francisco, CA: Jossey-Bass.

Radcliffe, S. (2012) *Leadership: Plain and Simple* (2nd edn). Harlow: Pearson.

Sherrington, T. (2015) Course correction: the leadership path is never straight, *Headguruteacher* (29 November). Available at: https://headguruteacher.com/2015/11/29/course-correction-the-leadership-path-is-never-straight/.

Sinek, S. (2009) How great leaders inspire action (video), *TED*. Available at: http://www.ted.com/talks/simon_sinek_how_great_leaders_inspire_action.

Thomson, P. (2009) *School Leadership: Heads on the Block?* London: Routledge.

Tomsett, J. (2015) *This Much I Know About Love Over Fear: Creating a Culture of Truly Great Teaching*. Carmarthen: Crown House Publishing.

Tough, P. (2012) *How Children Succeed*. London: Random House.

Tschannen-Moran, M. (2004) *Trust Matters: Leadership for Successful Schools*. San Francisco, CA: Jossey-Bass.

About the author

Dr Jill Berry taught for 30 years, between 1980 and 2010, holding seven different roles across six different schools. These included state and independent schools, comprehensive and selective schools, all boys', all girls' and co-educational schools, and 4–18, 7–18 and 11–18 schools. She has also taught GCSE and A level evening classes for adults. Jill was head of English, head of sixth form, deputy head and then head, a position she held for ten years.

Since 2010 Jill has completed a Professional Doctorate in Education, researching the transition from deputy headship to headship, as well as carrying out a range of leadership consultancy work. This includes consulting on the appointment of heads and senior leaders, appraisals and professional review, staff training, mentoring and coaching. She is also active within the online network of educators, tweeting @jillberry102, blogging via the platform @staffrm (http://staffrm.io/@jillberry) and writing for online and print media.

Jill is based in Newark in the Midlands.